BOOK 1

NEW HORIZONS

science 5-16

Key stage 3

CAMBRIDGE

BOOK 1

NEW HORIZONS

science 5~16

Key stage 3

CAMBRIDGE

Project development team

Jim Hudson
General Adviser (Science)

Jon Sargent
Formerly Advisory Teacher for Science

Wendy Jeffery
Formerly Advisory Teacher for Science

Authors

Garry Archer
St Paul's RC School, Haywards Heath

Joy Bannister
Warden Park School, Cuckfield

Robin Holloway
Steyning Grammar School

Wendy Jeffery
Formerly Advisory Teacher for Science

Jon Sargent
Formerly Advisory Teacher for Science

Julian Sims
Advisory Teacher for Science

Derek Slack
Advisory Teacher for Science

Introduction

A message from the authors of New Horizons

This book will help you with the work you will cover in science this year. It consists of four modules:

- *Laboratory matters*
- *Bodyworks*
- *Move it!*
- *Living and changing*

Although there are four separate titles, you will find that ideas from one also appear in others. Each spread contains some ideas for you to think about and to discuss with your friends and teacher, as well as suggestions for practical work. These are denoted by ■ in the text.
N.B. Where you see this symbol (left) you will need to take more care. If you are not sure why, ask your teacher.

In *New Horizons* there is great emphasis on practical work. We believe that being a scientist means doing science and understanding why you are doing that practical work. Scientists operate in very similar ways – going through the stages of describing a problem, making a plan, taking action to follow the plan, interpreting (or thinking about) their results and reporting what they have found out to other people.

You will practise these skills in the activities, rather in the way that a tennis player might practise one skill for a while before developing another.

In each module, there are investigations for you to undertake. An investigation is an activity with a difference. You will probably need most of the skills that you have practised. You will certainly need some of the knowledge about science that you have acquired, together with perseverance and determination to solve the problem and find an answer. Your teacher will encourage you to use the investigation prompt sheet to help you plan and carry out your task. At the end of the investigation, you may be required to report on it, perhaps by writing about it or by talking to your class.

We hope you will enjoy *New Horizons*. We liked writing the books, and the pupils of West Sussex enjoy using them! We believe that science is best understood by doing it and by talking about it. Through an understanding of science you will become more aware of the world around you and better able to use your knowledge and skills in real-life situations.

Contents

Laboratory matters

Being a scientist

What is science?

Science usually means knowing about the world around us. At school, you will investigate some of the questions that have puzzled scientists for a long time, such as:

- How do things fall?
- How does a human body work?
- What causes weather?
- Why do fish have gills?

Only recently have answers to questions like these been found. The exciting thing about science is that there is far more to be found out than we have already discovered! Perhaps there are some questions you would like to know the answers to.

A scientist working in the field

Working in a modern molecular biology laboratory

Who is a scientist?

Perhaps you have heard of geologists, astronomers and botanists.

- Can you find out what kind of science these people investigate and the sort of questions they ask?

There are many different kinds of scientist.

- Look at the pictures of scientists working.
- What do you think they are doing and where are they doing it?

All scientists have one thing in common; the way in which they work. It is called the 'scientific method'. In school you will learn how to work scientifically and you will use this method of working at home as well as at school.

As a scientist, you will learn the skills of science. You will learn to ask questions, make plans, carry out your plan safely, and interpret what you have found out. You will also need to report your discoveries. You will often have to work with other people. Scientists usually work in teams, so co-operation with other people is important.

Although the pictures show scientists working in a variety of places, you will do much of your science in a laboratory, because when gas, water and electricity are needed for investigations, this is the best place to be.

In this module, you will learn some of the skills of science and also about materials and how they are used.

Being safe and sensible

Careless behaviour in a laboratory can cause accidents. Your school laboratory will only be a safe place for working if everyone behaves sensibly and sticks to a few sensible rules.

- Look carefully at the picture.
- Discuss whether or not these pupils are behaving sensibly.
- What might happen to the pupils if they do not behave sensibly?

An astronomer at the controls of the 2.5 m Isaac Newton telescope on La Palma in the Canary Islands. The dotted line on the screen shows the path of light through the telescope

- Make a list of safety rules for your laboratory.
- Design and make a safety poster which tells other pupils about one of the rules.

Finding out about apparatus

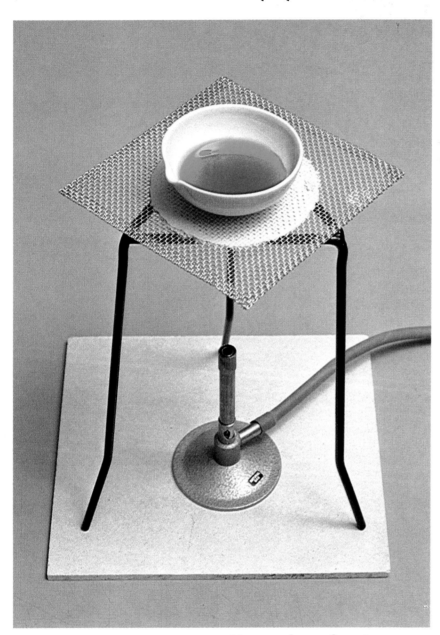

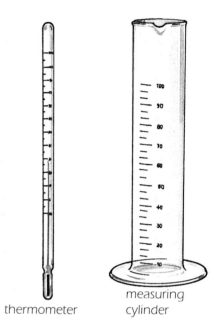

thermometer   measuring cylinder

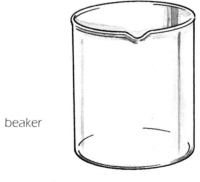

beaker

Name that piece!

The pictures show everyday scientific equipment, or apparatus. Use the pictures to name the items your teacher gives you. Later on, you will learn to handle them safely and with confidence.

Drawing apparatus

Scientists always make a record of their investigations.

Drawing a clear, accurate, labelled diagram is a good way of showing how apparatus is assembled and used.

Copymaster 1 shows how some pieces of apparatus are drawn.

■ Draw a clear, labelled diagram of the apparatus in the photograph.

Remember not to draw retort stands or heatproof mats.

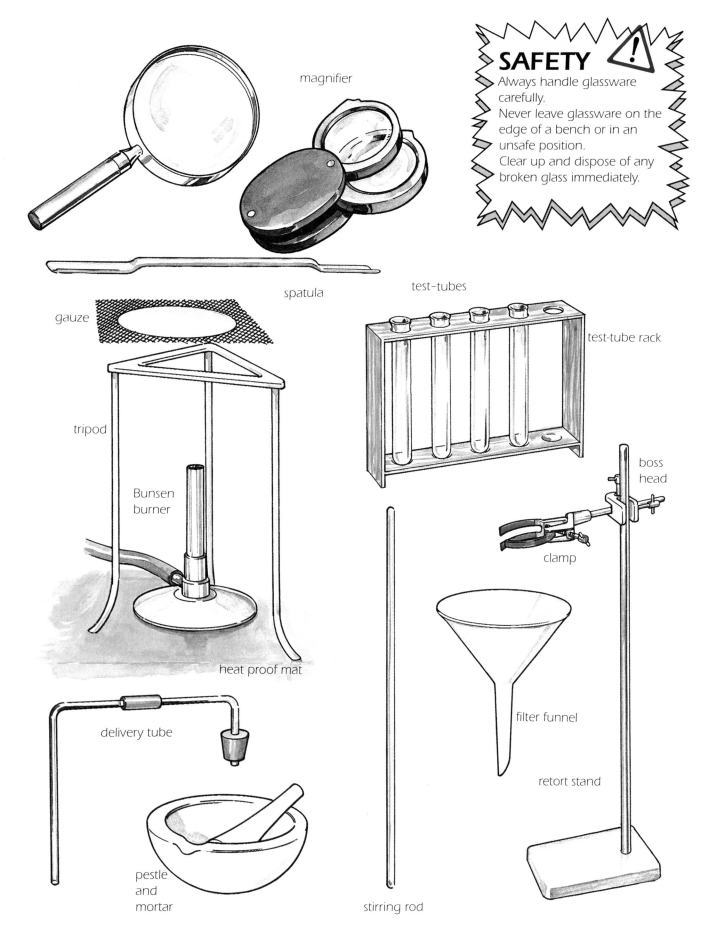

magnifier

spatula

test-tubes

gauze

test-tube rack

tripod

boss head

Bunsen burner

clamp

heat proof mat

filter funnel

delivery tube

retort stand

pestle and mortar

stirring rod

11

Heating things

Safe use of a Bunsen burner
in the laboratory

Until the year 1854, gas made from coal (coal gas) had been used mainly for lighting. Coal gas was not used for heating because its flame did not give out much heat.

In 1854, Robert Bunsen (1811–99), a German scientist, decided that a much hotter flame was possible. His idea was to mix air with coal gas just before it burned. This gave less light but more heat. The type of burner which does this is known as a Bunsen burner.

Bunsen burners now burn natural gas or calor gas.

Using a Bunsen burner

Three different types of flame are possible with a Bunsen burner.

The different flames are made by turning the collar.

Type of flame

| **Yellow flame** | **Medium flame** | **Roaring flame** |
| Air hole fully closed | Air hole half open | Air hole fully open |

Lighting the Bunsen burner

- Close the air hole.
- Light a splint.
- Apply the lighted splint from the side to the top of the burner, as shown below.
- Turn the gas on.

Your burner should be showing a yellow flame.

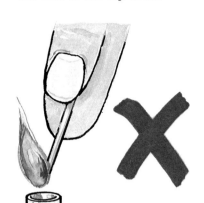
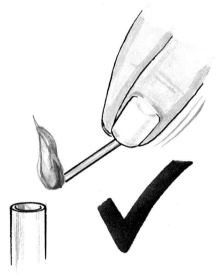

Which flame shall I use?

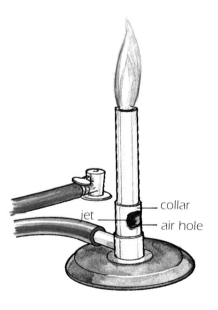

jet — collar
— air hole

- Set up the apparatus as shown on the opposite page.
- Light your Bunsen burner and adjust it to burn with a medium flame.
- Time how long it takes to boil a beaker containing 50 cm^3 of water using this flame.
- Remove the Bunsen burner and, when the beaker is cool enough to handle, exchange it for the next one.
- Repeat the experiment by adjusting your Bunsen burner to give a roaring flame.

Your teacher will perform the same experiment using the yellow flame.

- Put your results in a table like the one below.
- Draw a labelled diagram of your apparatus.
- Which flame was the best for heating the water?
- Why is the yellow flame sometimes called the safety flame?

Type of flame	Time taken to boil water	Other observations
Roaring		
Medium		
Yellow		

13

What is matter?

Everything in the world, including ourselves and all the things around us, is made of something which we call **matter** or **material.**

The buildings we live in, the clothes we wear, the food we eat, the water we drink and the air we breathe, are all made of matter.

Solids, liquids and gases

Matter can be found in three different forms or **states** – the solid state, the liquid state and the gas state.

■ Discuss what you think the words solid, liquid and gas mean.

Words such as 'hard', 'flexible' and 'runny' describe materials. Scientists call them the properties of the material. The statement 'glass is transparent' describes

the property (transparent) of the material (glass).

■ Can you think of some properties that all solids have?
■ What can you say about their size and shape?
■ Ask yourself the same question about liquids and gases.
■ How do you decide whether something is a solid, liquid or a gas?
■ Compare your ideas with those on **copymaster 2**

What's the state?

The picture shows objects made from different materials which have different properties. They can be sorted into groups using their properties.

When scientists sort things into different groups, they are **classifying** them.

Classifying helps scientists to identify patterns in their data.

■ Use your own ideas and the information on **copymaster 2** to classify the objects and materials you have been given as solids, liquids or gases.

■ Devise a way of recording your ideas.

Moving particles

Particle arrangement

You already know that solids, liquids and gases have different properties, but why do they behave as they do?

All matter is made of very tiny particles called **atoms**. These particles are so small that they cannot be seen, even through the most powerful optical microscope!

Although we cannot see them, we do know that these particles are always moving, sometimes slowly, sometimes more quickly.

In solids, particles are closely arranged in regular patterns and do not move about, although they do **vibrate** (move back and forth) slightly. This is why solids have a definite shape. Particles in liquids are not arranged in a regular way. They are free to move about, but they do stay close to each other. This is why liquids are runny and can be poured.

In a gas, the particles can move away from each other. They are able to move very quickly. They are not held close to other particles at all.

When a substance is heated, the particles in it move more quickly because they have more energy.

■ What do you think will happen to the particles when the substance cools down?

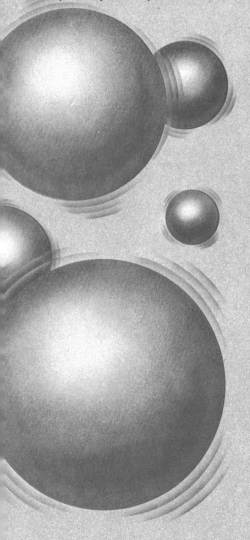

Handling substances

Only use small amounts of substances.

■ Observe the three substances you have been given carefully. How would you describe them?

■ Copy the table and record your observations in the first two columns.

Name of substance	Before heating	During heating	After heating (cool)

Heating a substance safely

Heating substances

The picture shows the correct way to heat substances.

■ Very gently heat a small amount of one of the substances in a boiling tube. Make sure you use the correct flame for gentle heating.

■ Observe what happens carefully. Allow the tube to cool before replacing it in the rack and continue to observe.

■ Record *all* your observations in the table.

■ Repeat the activity using the other substance.

Your teacher will heat a third substance for you to observe.

When substances change from one state to another as a result of heating or cooling we say they have 'changed state'. They are still the same substance and made from the same particles. **Copymaster 8** will help you to understand more about this.

■ Explain what you think has happened in the three substances that you heated using words like 'particles', 'heat', 'move', 'solid', 'liquid', 'gas', and 'state' to help you. Drawings may help your explanation.

17

Materials in the same or in different states are often mixed together. Some examples of mixtures are:

- gases: air – a mixture mainly of nitrogen and oxygen
- liquids: vinegar – a mixture of ethanoic acid and water
- solids: brass – a mixture of two metals, copper and zinc. A mixture of two metals is called an **alloy**. Use some other sources of information to find out more about alloys.

To separate substances from mixtures, we use our knowledge of their properties. One property of solid substances which is very useful for separating mixtures is its **solubility** or how easily it dissolves.

When sugar is mixed with water it dissolves. It is said to be soluble. Solids that do not dissolve are said to be **insoluble**.

- Discuss what you think happens to the particles of sugar when they dissolve in water.

Filtration

Filtration is a way of separating insoluble solids from liquids, using a **filter** or fine strainer. When peas are strained using a colander they are being separated from the water. This happens because the holes in the colander are smaller than the peas.

A coffee filter separates the solid coffee grains from the water. The filter paper has millions of tiny holes which are too small for large coffee grains to pass through. The tiny particles of coffee which give it its taste can pass through to flavour the water and make the coffee we drink.

- What is being filtered in the pictures above?

For filtering in the laboratory, we use a filter funnel and filter paper. We call the liquid which passes through the filter paper the **filtrate** and the solid which is left on the paper the **residue**.

Filtered out

- Set up the retort stand, filter funnel and conical flask as shown in the photograph.
- Wet the filter funnel.
- Fold the filter paper and place it in the funnel.
- Copy the table into your book.
- Pour 25 cm³ of the sandy water slowly into the filter paper. Do not let the water go over the top edge of the filter paper.
- Time how long it takes for the liquid to pass through the filter paper.
- Record your observations in the table.
- Using a new filter paper each time, repeat the experiment for the muddy water, the chalky water and the milk.
- Draw and label a diagram of the apparatus.
- Why do you think some mixtures take longer to separate than others?
- Why do you think the filter paper was unable to remove the white substance from the milk?

Mixture	Time for filtrate to pass through filter paper	Description of filtrate	Description of residue
Sandy water			
Muddy water			
Chalky water			
Milk			

Evaporation

Did you know?

Every day, 7.5 million tonnes of water evaporates from the Dead Sea.

Is tea a solution? What is the solute? What is the solvent?

Workers in Sri Lanka raking salt into piles as sea water evaporates from a shallow salt pan

Why do clothes dry more quickly on a windy day?

What happens when you dry your hair?

■ Discuss with your friends the most efficient way of getting your hair dry. What does drying your hair have in common with the other pictures on this page?

■ Look at **copymaster 8** and discuss with your friends what happens to the liquid water in the pictures above.

Dissolving

What happens to salt when it is added to water? It seems to disappear, but has it really? The salt has dissolved.

A solid that dissolves is called a **solute**. The liquid it dissolves in is called a **solvent**. The solute and solvent together are called a **solution**.

Separating salt

Seawater has common salt dissolved in it as well as other soluble substances.

In some dry parts of the world, people do not have an adequate fresh water supply. Some of them live near the sea.

■ What problems do these people have to overcome before they can use the sea to supply fresh water?

When salt dissolves in water, salt is the solute and water is the solvent.

■ Make a solution of common salt in water.

■ How could you separate the salt from the water?

■ Try out your ideas.

■ Write about what you have done.

■ Carry out the investigation on **copymaster 11**.

Separating pigments

Have you ever wondered why flowers are different colours or why people have different coloured eyes? Soluble substances called **pigments** are responsible for the colours of many things. You may have mixed paints to make different colours. The final colour is a mixture of different pigments. We can separate mixtures of pigments by a method called **chromatography.**

What colour is black ink?

- Half fill a beaker with water.
- Cut a strip out of a filter paper leaving the strip attached at the middle (see diagram).
- Using the end of a glass rod, put a small drop of ink in the middle of the filter paper. Allow it to dry.
- Place the filter paper over the top of the beaker, dipping the end of the strip into water.
- Watch what happens carefully and record your observations clearly and accurately.
- How many pigments did you separate from the black ink?

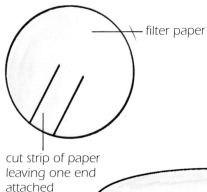
filter paper

cut strip of paper leaving one end attached

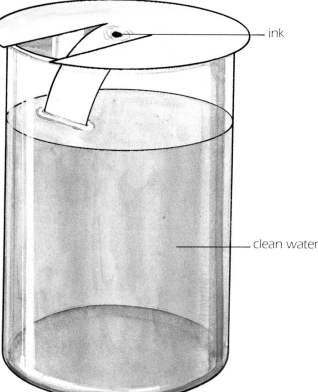
ink

clean water

LABORATORY MATTERS

Separating plant pigments

Not all plant pigments are soluble in water; some will only dissolve in other solvents such as ethanol and propanone.

In this activity, you will investigate which is the best solvent to dissolve different plant pigments.

■ Choose one part of a plant to investigate.

■ To extract the pigment, grind up the plant tissue in a pestle and mortar with a small volume of water and pour the liquid into a test-tube.

SAFETY ⚠
There must be no naked flames in the room during this activity.

■ Repeat using the other solvents instead of water.
■ How will you decide which is the best solvent?
■ How will you make sure your test is fair?
■ Devise an appropriate way to record your observations.
■ Report what happened during your investigation.

You could carry out the experiment using different plant parts.

■ Which is the best solvent for each of the pigments you have tested?
■ If plant pigments were soluble in water, what would happen when it rained?

Grinding plant tissue with a pestle and mortar

Acids and alkalis

There are many common substances that contain chemicals called **acids.** Acids give these substances their sharp, sour taste. You probably know that acids are corrosive. This means that they may attack and 'eat away' substances such as metals and may burn your skin. Vinegar contains ethanoic (acetic) acid. Lemons and grapefruit contain citric acid. A bee sting is acid.

One type of indigestion, called acid indigestion, is due to the presence of too much acid in the stomach. It can usually be cured by taking indigestion tablets which neutralise (or cancel out) the acid.

Neutralisers

In the laboratory, acids can be neutralised by chemicals called **alkalis.** Acids and alkalis can neutralise each other if they are mixed in the right amounts.

The table below gives some commonly used laboratory acids and alkalis. These colourless liquids are often used in experiments. You will understand more about them later in your course.

Common substances in the photograph (right) which form alkaline solutions when they dissolve in water. Can you name the substances they contain?

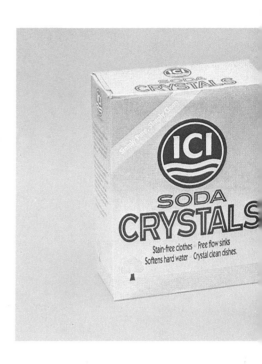

Name of acid	Name of alkali
hydrochloric acid	sodium hydroxide
sulphuric acid	calcium hydroxide
nitric acid	ammonium hydroxide (ammonia solution)

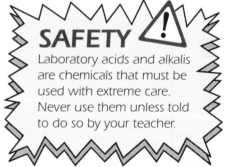

SAFETY ⚠️

Laboratory acids and alkalis are chemicals that must be used with extreme care. Never use them unless told to do so by your teacher.

Did you know?

The acid in the human digestive system is strong enough to dissolve an iron nail.

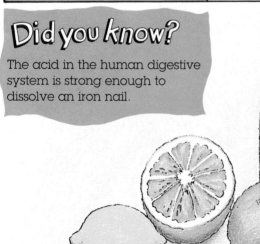

Common acidic substances. Can you name the acids they contain?

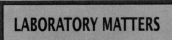

LABORATORY MATTERS

Indicators

Indicators are dyes that change colour when they are added to acids or alkalis. The first indicators used were natural dyes extracted from plants. Litmus is a dye which turns red in acid solutions and blue in alkaline solutions. Universal indicator is a mixture of several dyes. It produces a range of different colours when acids and alkalis are added to it. By matching the colour to a chart, we can see how strong an acid or alkali is.

pH and the pH scale

As well as using a scale of colours, we can use a scale of numbers, called the **pH scale**, to measure acid or alkali strength.

A neutral substance has a pH of 7. Acids have pH values below 7. Alkalis have pH values greater than 7.

Using universal indicator

- Your teacher will give you six test-tubes. Label them A to F.
- One quarter fill the tubes as follows:
  - **A** ammonium hydroxide
  - **B** citric acid
  - **C** sodium carbonate
  - **D** hydrochloric acid
  - **E** sulphuric acid
  - **F** distilled water
- Test each solution with universal indicator paper.
- Match the colour of the paper to the universal indicator chart to find the pH of each solution.
- Record your observations for each solution in the table.

Universal indicator colours and pH scale. (Look at your school universal indicator chart for accurate colours.)

Colour		pH	
red	1	strong	
orange	2		
	3		
	4	**acids**	
orange yellow	5		
yellow	6	weak	
yellowish green	7	neutral	
greenish yellow	8	weak	
green	9		
bluish green	10		
	11	**alkalis**	
blue	12		
	13		
violet	14	strong	

Solution	Colour of universal indicator paper	pH	Acidic or alkaline	Strength of acid or alkali
A				
B				
C				
D				
E				
F				

1.10

Measuring matter

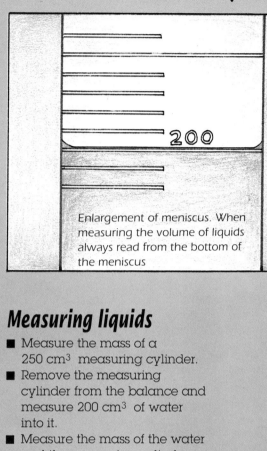

Enlargement of meniscus. When measuring the volume of liquids always read from the bottom of the meniscus

Measuring liquids

- Measure the mass of a 250 cm^3 measuring cylinder.
- Remove the measuring cylinder from the balance and measure 200 cm^3 of water into it.
- Measure the mass of the water and the measuring cylinder together. What is the mass of the 200 cm^3 of water? Show your calculations.
- Repeat your measurements using cooking oil instead of the water.
- Calculate the mass of 200 cm^3 of cooking oil.
- Compare the mass of the same volume of water and oil. Were they the same or different?
- Record what you have discovered.

Did you know?

Solids are not always denser than liquids. Ice is less dense than water. This is why icebergs float in the sea. Pumice, a kind of volcanic rock, can float on water too; the only rock to do so.

Measuring solids

You can also use a measuring cylinder in order to find the volume of a solid.
- Measure 50 cm^3 of water into a 100 cm^3 measuring cylinder. Place a pebble in the water and then read off the new volume.
- Calculate the volume of the pebble. Show your calculations.

Your teacher will provide blocks made from a range of materials.
- Measure the mass of each of the blocks.
- Use a similar method as before to find the volume of each of the solid blocks.
- Record all the data about the blocks in a table like the one shown below.
- What can you say about the volume of the blocks? Do they all have the same mass?

Block material	Volume (cm³)	Mass (g)

Materials which have the same volume may not have the same mass. You have seen that this is true for solids and liquids. Materials that have different masses for the same volume are said to differ in **density**. Water is denser than cooking oil. Why?
- Predict what will happen if you mix together water and cooking oil.
- Test your prediction and draw a labelled diagram to record your observations.
- Which of the blocks had the highest density? Look at the table to help you. How do you know this?
- Use your ideas about particles to explain why different materials have different densities.

Measuring gases

Your teacher will set up the apparatus and demonstrate this activity to you.
- What do you think will happen to the mass reading when the air in the container is removed using a vacuum pump?

Your teacher will carry out the evacuation.
- Can you explain what happens?
- What does this activity tell us about air? (Remember that air is a mixture of gases.)
- Report what happened in this activity to include an explanation of your observations.

The microscope

Bodyworks

The microscope is a very useful instrument. It makes things appear larger – in other words it magnifies. No-one is exactly sure who invented the microscope, but it was in use in Europe by about 1600.

Scientists of the time were very excited because they were able to see things that people had never seen before. They were keen to improve this new device so that they could see in even more detail.

Marcello Malpighi (1628–94) was born in Italy. He studied the lung of a frog under his microscope and discovered the tiny blood vessels that are known as capillaries.

In Holland, Anthony van Leeuwenhoek (1632–1723) developed a more powerful microscope through which he could see the smallest plants and animals in pond water.

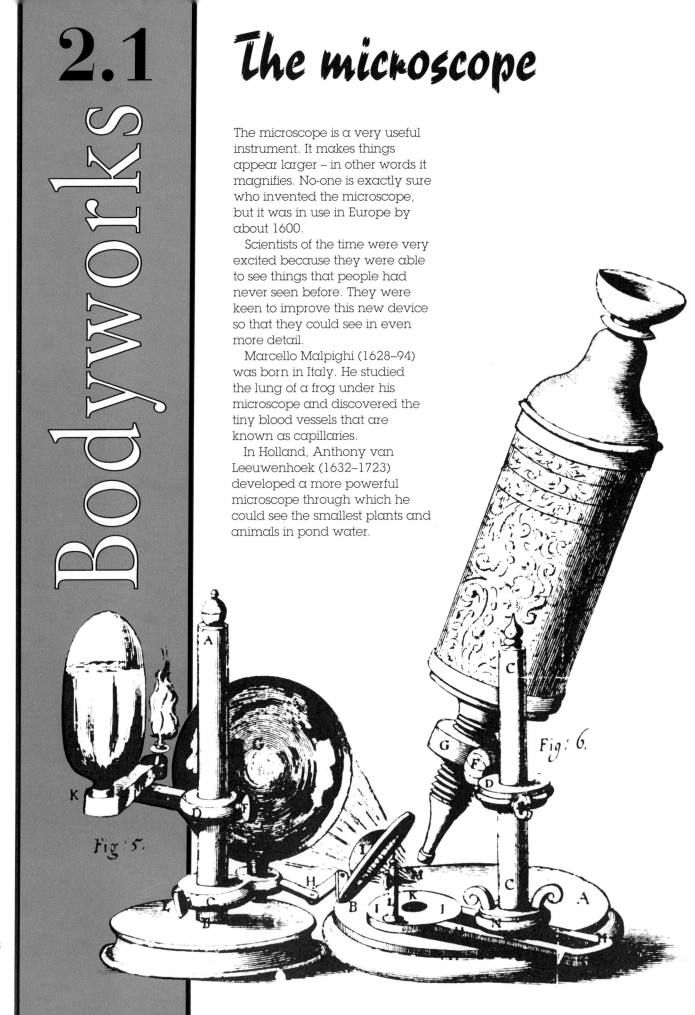

Fig: 5.

Fig: 6.

A microscope (left) made by English scientist Robert Hooke in 1663. Through his microscope, Hooke saw that cork was made up of small 'boxes', which he called cells (above)

Using a microscope

- Look at **copymaster 1**.
- Compare the microscope on the sheet with your own. You should learn the names of the different parts.
- If your microscope has a built-in light source, switch on the light. Otherwise, adjust the mirror until you can see the most light through the tube. You can now use your microscope to examine something from the selection your teacher will provide.
- Place what you have chosen to examine on a microscope slide.
- Put the slide on the stage so the material is over the hole and secure the slide with clips.

- Check that the nosepiece is turned to the low-power objective lens.
- Look from the side, with your eye level with the stage and, turning the focussing knob, bring the lens and the slide close together – make surethey do not touch!
- Now, look down the eyepiece and, turning the focussing knob, slowly move the objective lens away from the slide until you can see a clear image. The material on the slide is now in focus.

When you have finished, always leave your microscope clean and put it away.

You should adjust the mirror to the brightest position.

What are cells?

All living things are made up of tiny units called **cells.** Some animals are so small they are made of only one cell, but most **organisms** (living plants and animals) are made of many different cells. Most cells have certain things in common. Nearly all cells have a 'control centre' called a **nucleus** which controls everything going on in the cell.

The diagrams below show an animal cell and a plant cell. Although they both have a nucleus, there are some differences between them.

■ Which features do plant and animal cells have?
■ Which features do only animal cells have?
■ Which features do only plant cells have?

Features of cells

The **cytoplasm** is where the cell stores and makes chemicals.

The **cell membrane** holds the cell together. It is very thin and allows some food particles and oxygen to pass through it.

The **cell wall** of plant cells is a rigid structure around the cell. It allows most things to pass through it.

Chloroplasts are found in some plant cells. They contain chlorophyll, a green substance which allows the plant to trap light energy from the Sun. You will find out more about this later.

The **vacuole** is a space filled with a liquid called cell sap.

In the activity, you will find out more about cells. You will need to use a microscope to see them.

Not all animal and plant cells look exactly like the cells on the right. Other cells are shown on the next page.

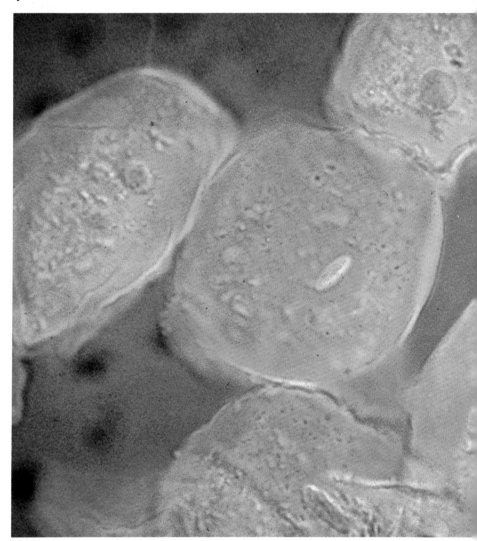

Cells from a human cheek, which have been stained and magnified about 200 times. The stain makes the cytoplasm appear green and the nuclei appear orange.

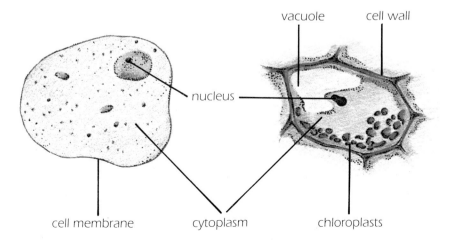

A human cheek cell

A pondweed cell

vacuole

cell wall

nucleus

cell membrane

cytoplasm

chloroplasts

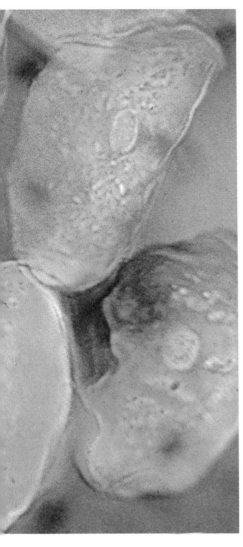

will need to alter the focussing knob only slightly
- Keep your slide.
- Repeat with another piece of onion skin on a second slide, but use iodine stain instead of water.
- Compare your two slides and make labelled drawings of what you see on each one. What did the iodine stain do?
- Look at your own slides of onion cells or slide of a human cheek cell. How are plant cells similar to animal cells? How do plant cells differ from animal cells?

Plant leaf cells

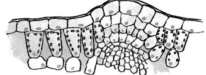

A bundle of human muscle cells

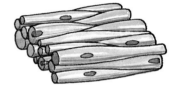

A human nerve cell

Looking at cells

- Peel off a small piece of thin skin from the inside of your piece of onion. Hold the skin by its edge.
- Lay the skin flat in the centre of a slide.
- Add a drop of water.
- Lower the cover slip on to the skin as shown in the diagram. Try to avoid trapping air bubbles.
- Examine your slide under the low-power objective lens of the microscope.
- Use a more powerful objective lens to have a closer look. You

1 Peeling off the skin

2 Laying the skin on a slide

3 Wetting the skin

4 Covering the skin

Cells, tissues and organs

We have already seen that all living things are made up of cells. The cells of the human body are like the inhabitants of a country. We need people with different abilities, or specialists, who play different roles in the running of the country. We need people who can govern, fight disease, remove waste, provide our food and transport, and so on. In the same way, our bodies need cells with special abilities.

In the body there are special cells with particular jobs to do. Cells of the same type join together to form different types of **tissue**, each with their own special jobs. For example, muscle cells form the tissue in the wall of the stomach and the gut.

These tissues in turn are built up into larger units called **organs**, such as the heart, the lungs, the brain or the stomach.

Organ systems

If you put some organs together to carry out an important process in your body, such as digestion, you have an **organ system**. The digestive system consists of the gullet, stomach, small and large intestine, rectum and anus.

All the organs and organ systems together make up an independent, living thing.

The organ systems carry out all the functions which are necessary for us to live.

You have already looked at some plant cells. Plant cells also make up tissues and organs which have special functions. You will find out more about these later in this course.

How many millions of cells do you think make up the body of this weightlifter?

BODYWORKS

Bodybuilding

- Cut out the outline of the body on **copymaster 2**.
- Cut out the organs, organ systems, skull and rib-cage.
- Place the organs, organ systems, skull and rib-cage in the correct position on your body outline. You may need to use books to help you. Think before you glue. Some organs will need to go on top of others.
- What is the main function of the skull and rib-cage?
- Now stick the body you have made into your book.
- Label the main organs and organ systems.

What is health?

People seem to find it much easier to talk about their illnesses than about being in good health. Next time you are in a queue, listen to the grown-ups' conversations around you. If they are talking about health, they will probably be discussing what's wrong with them – their aches and pains.

This isn't because people are naturally miserable, or even because they are particularly unhealthy. It's because illness is much easier to talk about than healthiness. Being healthy means different things to different people. What do you mean by 'health' and 'being healthy'?

The next activity will help you to decide what being healthy really means.

Have you got a healthy attitude?

Although we cannot control all the things that affect our health, there are many that we do have some control over.
- Think of all the things that might affect your health now and later in your lifetime.
- Divide these things into two lists under the headings:

Things that I CAN control
Things that I CANNOT control

Here is a list of features which could be used to describe a healthy person:
- is never ill
- does not drink alcohol
- gets up easily in the morning
- likes to play sports

THE MEDICINE WORKED A **TREAT,** I WAS UP AND ABOUT THE **NEXT** DAY! HOW'S **YOUR** FOOT, IS IT ANY **BETTER**?

I'VE HAD THE 'FLU – THE WHOLE **FAMILY** HAS BEEN ILL, AND **NOW** BILLY'S ILL IN BED! HOW'S YOUR LOT?

OH, MY BACK'S KILLING ME IT **MUST** HAVE BEEN TRYING TO SHIFT THAT FURNITURE YESTERDAY – IF IT GETS WORSE I'M OFF TO BED!

- does regular exercise
- does not smoke
- has good teeth
- is strong
- recovers quickly from illness
- is not overweight
- has a good appetite
- is always alert
- has never been in hospital
- does not need to take medicine

■ Discuss the list with a small group of friends and choose five features which you think are the most important.

■ Present your group's ideas to the class by a method of your own choice.

■ Devise a way to summarise the class ideas for this activity.

■ Record which feature was the most popular choice.

Does regular exercise help to keep you healthy?

Food for thought

There are many foods on sale at a market. Some are produced locally, and some come from other countries. Which do you think are local products?

'I'm starving!' People often say this when they are feeling hungry. What is hunger? Is it our body trying to tell us something?

Why do we need food?

We can classify foods into two main groups:
- those which help us to grow and repair the parts of our body that get damaged
- those which give us energy and help us to keep warm.

Growth foods

These contain **proteins.** Proteins are chemicals which your body uses to build up new cells and tissues. Sources rich in proteins are meat, fish, cheese, eggs, milk, nuts and beans.

Foods for energy and warmth

These contain **carbohydrates** and **fats**. They provide the fuel for all our body activities. Sugar and starch are carbohydrates. Sources rich in carbohydrates are bread, potatoes, rice and bananas. Fats are found in butter, cheese and meat.

Fats are easily stored in the body and carbohydrates will be converted to fat if not used up. Fats in the diet may be deposited in the blood vessels and could eventually cause strokes and heart attacks.

■ What do you think happens if you eat more carbohydrates than your body needs? What happens if you eat less? Find out the meaning of 'malnutrition'.

Can you match the items on the left with the main groups of food they contain?

What more do we need to eat?

As well as carbohydrates, fats and proteins our body needs small quantities of **vitamins** and **minerals.**

■ Find out about these substances and why they are important in keeping us healthy.
■ Discuss why young people need lots of protein.

What's in it?

■ Use **copymaster 4** to carry out tests on your food samples. There are four **food tests:**
   Test 1 for **STARCH** (a type of carbohydrate)
   Test 2 for **GLUCOSE** (a type of sugar)
   Test 3 for **PROTEIN**
   Test 4 for **FAT**
■ Record your results in a table like the one below.
■ Devise a way to classify your foods and clearly show any obvious patterns in your data.

Test	Food	Observation (tick if substance is present; cross if not present)

BALANCED DIET
A balanced diet should contain foods from each of these groups:
Protein
Fat
Carbohydrates
Vitamins
Minerals
Roughage
Water

A healthy diet

Look at the label

All packaged foods have a list of ingredients on the packet. They are listed in order of weight, the main ingredient at the top. Also, any food additives are listed on the label.

■ Why are these substances added to foods?

Your homework will help you to find out more about the different foods you eat.

Colours

■ Take three Smarties of different colours.
■ Moisten them with a drop of water and place each one on a piece of filter paper.
■ Remove them. What do you see? Label the colours in pencil. Replace the Smarties.

■ Add drops of water slowly on top of the Smarties.
■ Describe what you see.
■ What is the name of the method you have used?
■ How do you think the colouring for different Smarties might be made?
■ Why do food manufacturers add colouring to food?
■ Discuss with your friends whether you think colourings are really necessary?

Flavours

■ Work in pairs for this activity. You should both wash your hands before starting. One person should set up the test without the other person seeing the set-up.

■ Put two crisps, taken from the same packet, each on a clean piece of paper and label them 'A' and 'B'.
■ Put one crisp from another packet on a third piece of paper and label this one 'C'.
■ Now, ask your 'taster' to hold his or her nose and taste each crisp. Can he or she identify the odd one out?
■ Repeat the experiment without holding noses.
■ What is a flavour?

How sweet!

You should know by now that too many sweet foods are bad for your teeth. Tiny living things, called **microorganisms,** which are in your mouth can breed very fast. They feed on the bits of food left on your teeth and they love sugar most of all.

   If you do not clean your teeth, a sticky film called plaque builds up. It contains the sugar, the microorganisms and the acid they produce. This acid eats away the surface of teeth and tooth decay is the result.

■ List as many ways as you can to keep your teeth healthy.

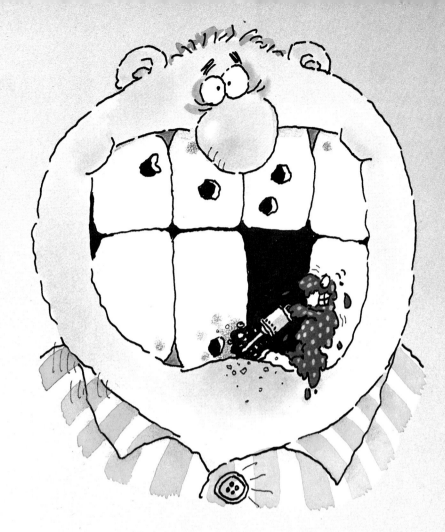

Would you include any of these foods in a healthy diet?

What happens to your food?

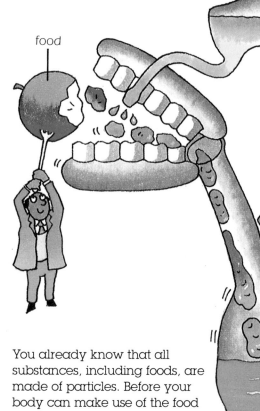

food

saliva

enzymes

Breaking down the food

Saliva makes the food easier to swallow. It also contains a chemical substance called an **enzyme,** which turns starch from the food into sugar. Sugar and starch are both carbohydrates but sugar particles are smaller than starch particles.

enzymes

stomach

small intestine

You already know that all substances, including foods, are made of particles. Before your body can make use of the food you eat, the food must be broken down into these particles. We call this process **digestion.**

Digestion begins in the mouth. As we chew our food, it is broken into smaller pieces. A liquid called saliva is mixed with it. It is saliva which makes our mouths water when we think about something nice to eat!

food particles

Nearly all digested food passes into the blood from the small intestine

bloodstream

Once the food is in the bloodstream, the blood takes it to the cells all over the body

used blood

kidneys remove waste liquid from blood

Your digestive system is like this imaginary machine. Food enters the system at one end and passes along a tube where it is broken down or digested. There are three main sections: stomach, small intestine, large intestine

clean blood

The food travels on through the stomach and intestines. As it travels, more enzymes break down the carbohydrates, proteins and fats into smaller units. Eventually, the food particles are small enough to pass through the wall of the intestine into the bloodstream. The blood then takes the food to the cells all over the body.

Digestion means breaking food into particles small enough to enter the bloodstream.

Food that you cannot digest collects in the rectum and is passed out through the anus. In a healthy diet, much of this is fibre and is present in plant foods such as fruit and vegetables. It helps food move through the digestive system.

The plastic gut

You are going to make a model of your intestines out of a piece of plastic tubing! In real life, your intestines would stretch for about 7 m if unravelled, but the tubing will act in some ways exactly like your intestines.

■ Tie a knot at one end of the special plastic (visking) tubing.
■ Open the other end and, using a dropper, half fill it with starch suspension.
■ Add a few drops of enzyme solution.
■ Tie a knot in the other end.
■ Put the tubing into a boiling tube and almost fill the boiling tube with warm, distilled water.
■ After 20 min, remove the plastic tubing.
■ Divide the water in the boiling tube into two test-tubes.
■ Test one for starch and the other for sugar. (Use **copymaster 4** to help you.)

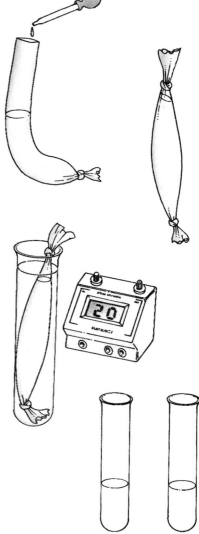

■ Test the contents of the visking tubing in the same way.
■ Record your observations.
■ What has happened to the starch inside the tubing?
■ Why is starch unable to enter the bloodstream?
■ How do enzymes help digestion?

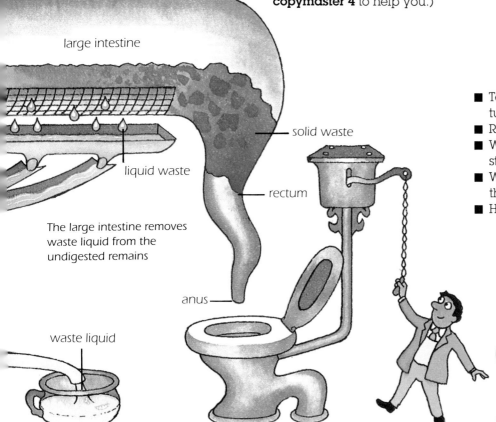

large intestine

solid waste

liquid waste

rectum

The large intestine removes waste liquid from the undigested remains

anus

waste liquid

Did you know?

Food stays in your stomach between one and a half and four hours. A meal takes about a day to travel right through you.

41

2.8 How do plants get their food?

Seaweed at low tide

Moss plant with spore containers

Plants also need food to grow and produce energy, but they don't have a digestive system like yours.

So, how do plants get their food? You probably have some ideas about this already. In the next activity, you will be able to share your ideas with your friends and discuss your ideas as well as theirs.

You will then be able to test those ideas – scientists do this all the time.

How does your garden grow?

- Discuss with a group of friends how you think plants get their food.
- Make a poster to illustrate your group's ideas.
- With your teacher, list all the ideas which appear on your class posters.
- Choose one of the ideas from the list which you can test.

- To test your idea, plan and carry out an investigation.
- Produce another poster to illustrate your investigation.
- Discuss with your friends whether your ideas are the same as they were before you carried out the investigation.
- Compare your ideas with the information given on **copymaster 8.**

House plants: parlour palm (left) and ladder fern (right and back)

An oak tree in a spring meadow

43

What happens to the air you breathe?

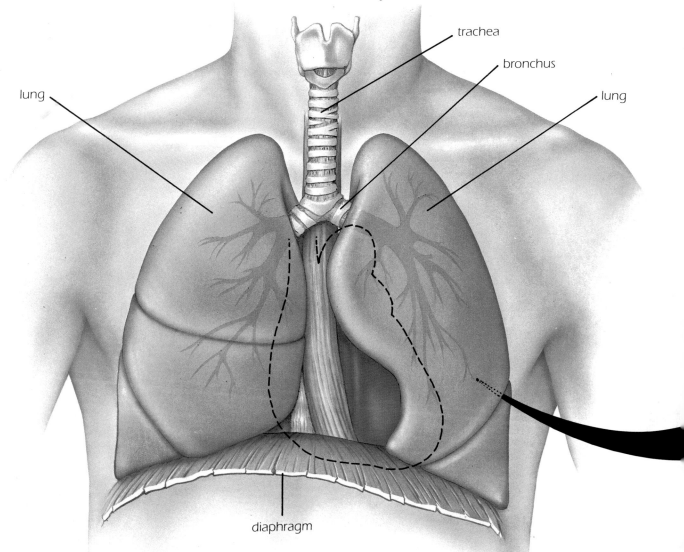

trachea

bronchus

lung

lung

diaphragm

You know that we need carbohydrates for energy, but we can only get this energy if we 'burn' carbohydrates by combining them with oxygen in our cells.

To get this oxygen, we need to breathe in air. When you breathe in, you increase the size of your chest by movements of your rib cage and a sheet of muscle below your ribs called the diaphragm.

Respiration

Air enters your nose or mouth and passes down the windpipe, or trachea. Each lung is connected to the windpipe by a tube called a bronchus. Inside the lung, this tube divides many times. The smallest tubes end in a group of air sacs called alveoli. Blood flows around these air sacs. It collects oxygen from them, and carries it to all the

cells of the body. Sugars from digested carbohydrates and the oxygen you breathe in meet in the cells. There they combine to produce energy to keep the body working.

The waste products of this reaction are the gases carbon dioxide and water vapour. These pass into the blood and are breathed out of the lungs. This whole process is called **respiration.**

Remember the respiration process, because you will need to write a word equation at the end of the next activity.

Breathe in!

- Put your hands on your ribs and breathe in as deeply as you can. Which way do your ribs move?
- With a partner, measure the size of your chest after taking a deep breath and again after breathing out.

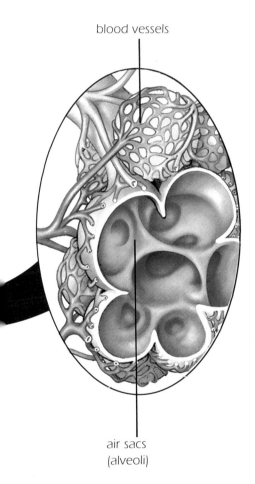

blood vessels

air sacs
(alveoli)

When you breathe in, your ribs move outwards, causing air to be sucked into your lungs

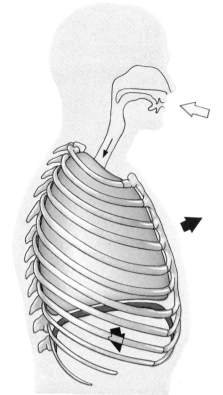

When you breathe out, your ribs move inwards, causing air to be squeezed from your lungs

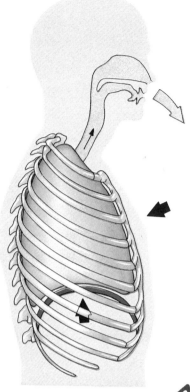

- Record your measurements in a table like this:

Size of my chest after breathing in	
Size of my chest after breathing out	

- How much bigger is your chest when you breathe in? The increase in chest size is called your chest expansion.

- Fill a 5 dm³ plastic container with water and then screw on the top.
- Turn the container upside down into a bowl of water.
- Remove the top under water and put one end of a rubber tube into the container.

- Take a deep breath and blow into the other end of the tube.
- Mark the new water level on the container.
- Empty the container completely, then measure how much water is needed to fill the container up to your mark. Use a 500 cm³ beaker for this.
- How much air can your lungs hold? We call this your lung capacity.
- Write the word equation for respiration, filling in the boxes with the words given.

**energy   sugar   oxygen
water vapour   carbon dioxide**

45

2.10 Smoking

COLLECT YOUR COUPON BUTTS

BUTTS

BUTTS COLLECT YOUR COUPON FOR BRONCHITIS

BUTTS COLLECT YOUR COUPON FOR CANCER

LOW TO MIDDLE TAR A

Warning: SMOKING CAN CAUSE

Health Department

DON'T GET TO MIDDLE AGE AND SAY BUTT IF ONLY I HADN'T...

Just say 'no'!

Have you ever been offered a cigarette? Write down where it was and who offered it to you. If not, think what you would do if you were offered a cigarette.

■ Get into a group, with three or four friends.

■ Your task is to act out a short sketch about smoking.
■ Decide who will play these roles: a smoker; one or two very tempted non-smokers, one or two definite non-smokers.
You will have a 'quiet time' to study your role.

■ Get your group together again. Decide upon your situation: in the school playground; on the bus home, for example.
■ Each group will present their sketch to the class.
■ Discuss these questions:
In what ways are you encouraged to smoke?
Should cigarette advertising be allowed?
Do you think smoking should be banned in public places?

If someone asked you to breathe in a mixture of irritating, poisonous and cancer-causing substances, would you do it? Such substances are found in tobacco, so why do people smoke?

People start to smoke for all kinds of reasons. Young children may copy older brothers or sisters, teenagers may smoke because their friends do – they want to 'fit in' or appear 'grown-up'. Older people may have become smokers before the dangers were known. Now they are addicted to a drug called nicotine, present in tobacco. Nicotine is habit-forming and smokers' bodies and minds depend upon it.

Smoking gives you bad breath, stained teeth and dull, wrinkled skin. It causes coughs and chest infections. Cigarette smoke leaves a sticky deposit of tar in your lungs, which can cause cancer. Lung cancer kills more than 40 000 people every year in the UK and 90% of these are smokers.

Passive smoking means breathing in the smoke of other people's cigarettes.

The children of smokers get more lung illnesses than other children. Why is this?

efined by H.M. Government
LUNG CANCER & HEART DISEASE
hief Medical Officers

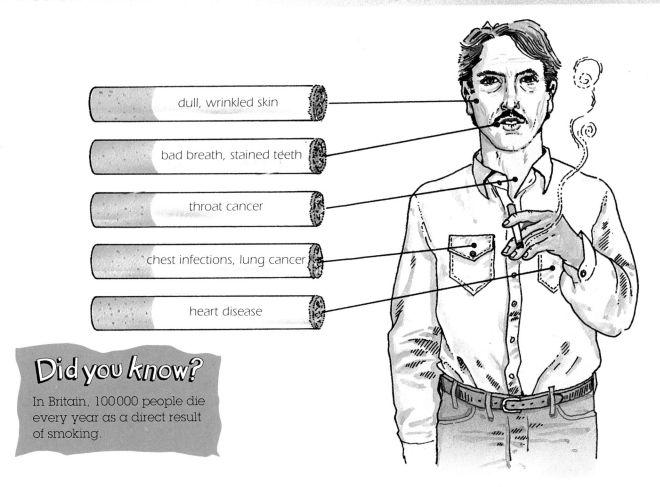

dull, wrinkled skin

bad breath, stained teeth

throat cancer

chest infections, lung cancer

heart disease

Did you know?

In Britain, 100 000 people die every year as a direct result of smoking.

Blood circulation: the transport system

You know that your cells need food and oxygen which are carried in your blood. How does the blood get round your body?

First circuit

Blood is pumped round the body by the heart. The heart beats between 45 and 70 times a minute. The blood leaves the heart through tubes called **arteries** which take the blood to all parts of the body. The arteries divide into tiny tubes called **capillaries** which pass through your tissues and take food and oxygen to the cells.

The blood travels back to the heart, first in capillaries and then in larger vessels called **veins.**

Second circuit

The blood then begins a second circuit – through the lungs. In the lungs, the waste carbon dioxide leaves the blood and is breathed out. The red blood cells collect fresh oxygen. The blood returns to the heart ready for another circuit round the body.

Heart disease in adults usually occurs because arteries get clogged up with a fatty substance from the blood. If one of the arteries supplying the heart with blood becomes completely blocked, the person will have a heart attack. In Britain, heart disease kills more people than any other illness.
- Look back at the activity on spread 2.5.
- Discuss how you can keep your heart healthy.

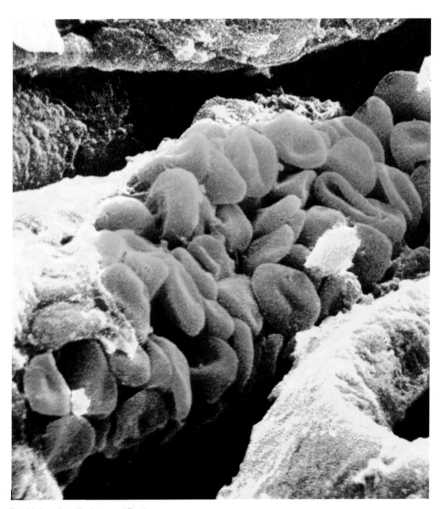

Red blood cells (magnified 600 times) in a capillary. The photograph is coloured so that the blood cells appear red and the capillary walls appear green

William Harvey 1578–1657

In 1625, Harvey discovered that blood circulated round the body. Before that, people thought that blood passed back and forth in two separate parts of the body.
- Find out more about Harvey's discovery, his life and the times in which he lived.

Did you know?

- Your heart beats about 100 000 times a day.
- It takes 60 s for blood to make a complete circuit round your body.
- There are about 100 000 km of blood vessels in your body.

BODYWORKS

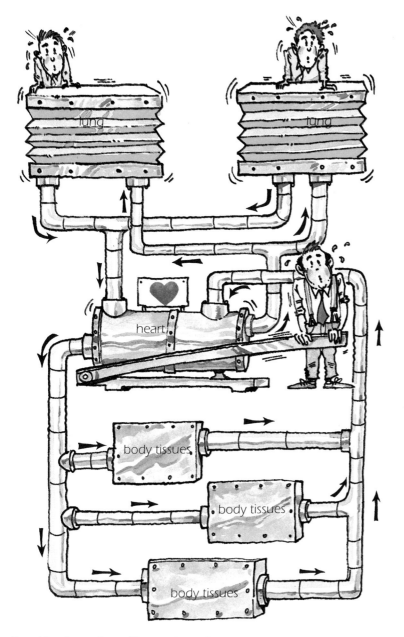

Your blood vessels are like a system of pipes. The heart pumps blood to the body tissues, and then it returns to the lungs

Feel the pulse in a friend's wrist using the tip of your middle finger. What is his or her pulse rate?

- Now do 2 min vigorous exercise. Your teacher may make some suggestions.
- Measure your pulse rate straight away after the exercise.
- Keep measuring your pulse rate for 1 min every 2 min until it returns to normal.
- Devise a way to record your results. Draw a line graph to show your pulse rate before and after exercise.

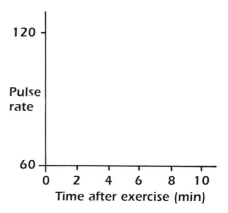

- How long did it take for your pulse rate to return to normal (the average pulse rate worked out at the beginning)? People who take a lot of exercise and are fit recover quickly. Their pulse rate returns to normal more rapidly than those who are less fit.

   It may be interesting to compare your recovery rate with others in your class.

Finger on the pulse

- Hold one hand out palm upwards.
- Place the tip of the middle finger of your other hand on your wrist, as shown in the photograph.
- When you have found your pulse, count the number of beats in 1 min. This is your pulse rate.
- Repeat this twice and record all three figures.

- Find the average pulse rate. Add the three figures and divide by three.

	Pulse rate
1	
2	
3	
Total	
Average pulse rate (total ÷ 3)	

How your body moves

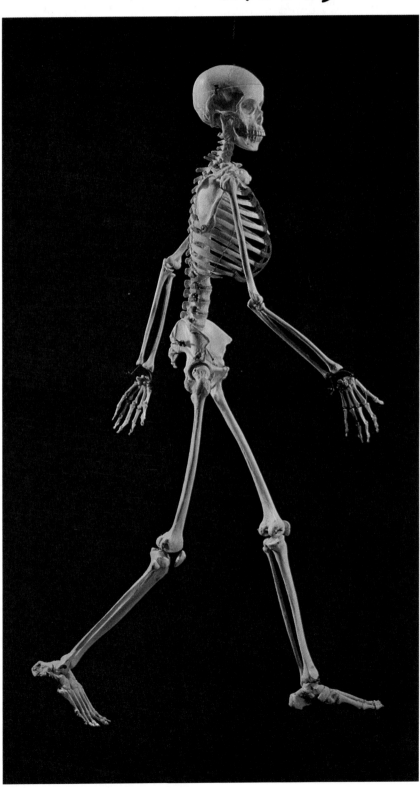

The human skeleton is built up of more than 200 bones which support and protect the body organs from injury. The bones also provide a solid base for the muscles to work against.

The bones of the skeleton meet at many joints. Some are fixed joints, allowing no movement. Other joints allow us to move in various ways. **Copymaster 11** shows four types of joint and how they work.

Muscle control

Movements occur when we contract muscles. Muscles are a special type of tissue which is elastic. There are two main types. Involuntary muscles are normally controlled by the brain with no continuous effort. The muscles involved in breathing and heart beating are of this type. Voluntary muscles are those which we are able to control at will.

A human skeleton

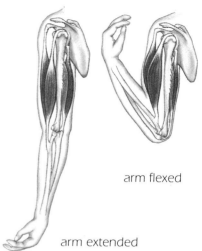

arm flexed

arm extended

To bend your arm, the large muscle at the top, called the biceps, shortens. The muscle under the arm lengthens

Movement and me

- Work with a partner for this activity.
- Copy this table into your book.
- Either you or your partner should try to keep absolutely still for 5 min.
- The other one should watch carefully and record any movement, no matter how small, in the table.

- Swop over and repeat the activity.
- Discuss with your partner what sorts of movements each of you made during the activity. Were they voluntary or involuntary?

What moved	Description of movement e.g. up, down, turn, etc.	Movement group	What useful job the movement does

Move those bones!

You are going to examine three different types of joint movements in your own skeleton.

- Type **A** joints allow movement in one direction (or plane) only – like the hinge on a cupboard door.
- Type **B** joints allow movement in two different directions.
- Type **C** joints allow sliding movement.

Use **copymaster 11** to help you.

- Devise a way to record all the different movements that your skeleton can make.
- Sort all the movements into types **A**, **B**, **C**.
- Choose a way to present all this information so that you can show how many of the different types of movement there are in your body.

2.13

How fit are you?

Exercise helps make your body healthy, fit and strong.

When you exercise, your heart beats faster, your breathing is faster and you feel tired but, the fitter you are, the quicker you will recover.

Strength and stamina

Muscles will waste away if they are not used, but regular exercise will build them up, increasing their size and strength. Exercise increases the stamina of muscles. This means that they get used to physical effort and do not tire quickly after a short burst of activity.

Suppleness and general health

If joints are not stretched regularly, they will become stiff. Exercise keeps them supple. Regular exercise improves your appetite, helps digestion and

reduces your chances of future heart diseases. Exercise helps to keep you fit.

A low pulse rate is a sign of fitness. Unfit people with high pulse rates should not suddenly take vigorous exercise. They should follow a sensible programme of exercise and increase their fitness over a period of time.

Swimming is a good, all-round exercise

■ Carry out the investigation on **copymaster 12.**

52

BODYWORKS

These people are all exercising their bodies in day-to-day activities – how do you get your exercise?

Message received

Our bodies are receiving messages from our surroundings all the time. What messages are you receiving now? How does your body interpret them? How do you react to them?

Your central nervous system consists of the brain, the spinal cord and the nerves.

Your brain controls all your activities. You do not even have to think about some of them, like breathing or blinking for example! The brain also receives messages from your eyes, ears and other sense organs.

Sending signals

Your spinal cord is an extension of your brain. From it, nerves branch off to reach all parts of your body.

Your brain reacts to messages received by sending signals back to the muscles. Different parts of the brain receive different types of message. You react so quickly that sometimes you don't have time to think. What would happen if you picked up a hot test-tube by mistake? This type of reaction is called a reflex action.

Voluntary actions are actions over which you have control.
■ Are the following actions reflex or voluntary: blinking; laughing; picking up a pencil; sneezing; scratching?

Your brain is like a computer. It receives messages carried along nerves in your body and spinal cord. Information from your eyes, ears and nose is also sent to your brain for processing

How do you react?

How quickly do you think your nerves send messages to your brain and back again to your muscles? The time taken is your reaction time.

- Work in pairs. Your partner will hold a metre rule vertically so that the end (zero mark) is between your first finger and thumb. The ruler must not touch your finger or thumb.
- Look at the zero mark on the ruler – your partner will drop it when you are not expecting it! You must not look at him or her for clues.
- When the ruler is dropped, catch it as quickly as you can.
- Make a note of the distance the ruler drops. Use the graph on **copymaster 13** to change the distance into a time. What is this time?
- Repeat this five times and work out an average.
- Change partners and repeat the experiment.

- Can you think of ways of reducing the time taken to catch the ruler?
- Try any ideas you have for shortening the time.
- Do you think that tiredness may affect your reaction time? How?
- Test your idea.

Did you know?

- Messages passing to and from the brain travel as fast as some racing cars (200 mph).
- Some nerve cells stretch the entire length of the spinal column. They are more than 1 m long, making them the longest cells in the body.
- The average human brain weighs about 1400 g and has 14 000 000 000 nerve cells.

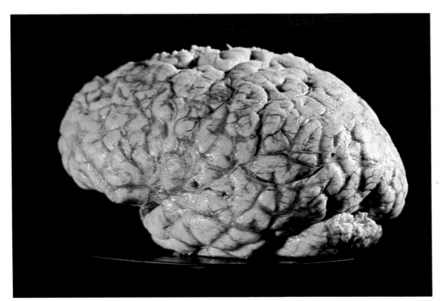

Adult human brain

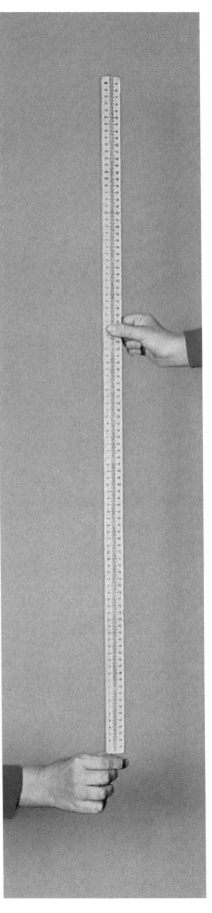

A habit is something we do regularly. Some habits are healthy and safe, for example cleaning our teeth or looking both ways before crossing the road. Other habits are bad for us; some may be deadly. A habit that is difficult to give up is called addiction.

People can be addicted to a variety of substances. Smoking, drinking alcohol, taking drugs and sniffing glue or solvents are all addictive. Any of these substances can damage your body and affect your mind.

Alcohol abuse

Having a drink seems to be very adult, yet alcohol can cause great damage to people and their families. Many road accidents are due to people who have drunk too much. When you drink too much it is difficult to judge speed and distance – both vital if you are to drive safely. Alcohol can make people lose their self-control and do things that they would never do if they were sober. Many fights start because people drink too much.

In the UK, over one million people are drinking alcohol at levels which will seriously damage their health

Many young people have died from sniffing substances like glue and aerosols.

■ Discuss with your friends why people sniff glue, use drugs or drink alcohol.
■ Do you think you can 'just try it once and get away with it?'

BODYWORKS

Harmful habits

Part 1

■ On **copymaster 14** choose five of the influences listed and then fill in the boxes.

■ Check and discuss your decisions with a partner.

Part 2

We come across solvents every day. What is a solvent?

Most solvents are harmless, but some give off vapours (gases) which can be harmful. When you sniff these vapours, they pass into your lungs and then into your blood. What might happen next?

■ Read the passage above from the *Daily Horizon*.

11 YEAR OLD GIRL DIES AFTER GLUE-SNIFFING

An 11 year old girl died today after experimenting with glue-sniffing for the first time. The girl, named only as Lynda, was at a party with a group of friends at the time of her death. One of the group told police that Lynda had been called 'chicken' because she would not join in the glue-sniffing at first. Eventually, she was persuaded to. She passed out and vomited. She then choked to death on her own sick.

■ Draw a storyboard similar to those you have seen in magazines. Make a series of about six drawings which illustrate the story of Lynda and her friends. Give not only their words, but also their thoughts.

■ Consider these two points and include them in your storyboard – they may alter the ending of the story:
How could Lynda's friends have helped her?
What is meant by 'peer group pressure'? How can this influence the decisions that people make?

Defend yourself!

Microorganisms are so small that we can only see them by using a powerful microscope. Many of them are useful in the production of foods like cheese and yogurt. Some microorganisms can cause disease and these are often called 'germs'.

Bacteria

Bacteria are microorganisms consisting of a single cell. Many live in our bodies and cause us no harm. Others can make us very ill if they enter the body. Microorganisms which cause disease are called **pathogens**. Sore throats, stomach upsets and more serious diseases like typhoid and tuberculosis are caused by bacteria. Bacteria reproduce by dividing in two, this can happen every 20 min. So large numbers of bacteria are produced quickly.

Viruses

Viruses are even smaller than bacteria. One million could fit into a single bacterium! An especially powerful microscope called an electron microscope is needed to see a virus. Viruses may cause diseases in plants and animals. The common cold, influenza, measles, and AIDS are all caused by viruses.

Bacteria like these exist in the nose and throat and on the skin of healthy people

Your defence force

When microorganisms enter your body, white blood cells are produced. These are your body's defence force. Some white cells eat pathogens and destroy them. Others produce chemicals called antibodies which destroy the pathogens. When antibodies are produced to fight one particular disease, they may remain in

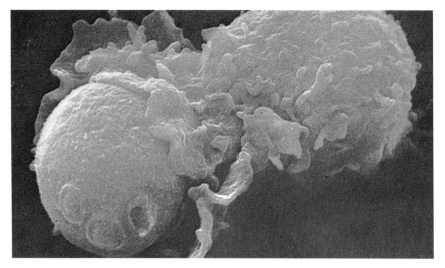

A photograph from an electron microscope coloured to show a white blood cell engulfing a foreign cell. This process is called phagocytosis and is part of the body's defence system

Some types of bacteria

Staphylococcus
(can cause boils)

Streptococcus
(can cause sore throats)

rod-shaped bacillus
(some can cause diseases)

your body and protect you from that disease in the future. You are then said to be immune to that disease.

Doctors can immunise people against some diseases. They give the patient a vaccine containing weak or dead microorganisms which cause a particular disease. By producing the right antibodies, your body is prepared to fight that disease in the future. Which diseases have you been immunised against?

Diseases that are passed from person to person are called infectious. You may have heard people say that a 'bug' is going around. What does this mean?

■ Carry out a survey of the infectious diseases that members of your class have had. Choose a good way to record and display the results of your survey.

Did you know?

The smallest independently-living thing is a bacterium living in sewage. Ten thousand of these bacteria side by side would measure only 1 mm.

What's bugging you?

If you have ever had influenza or 'flu, chickenpox or any other infectious disease, you may remember that your body temperature was high. This is one of the symptoms of fever and is a sign that your body is fighting the disease.

■ Look at the graph of body temperature and illness.
■ Copy it into your book. Write the words 'fever', 'recovery', and 'infection' in the correct place on the graph.

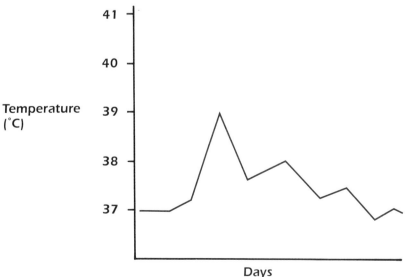

Body temperature and illness

Temperature (°C)

Days

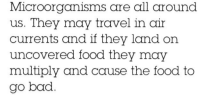

Microorganisms are all around us. They may travel in air currents and if they land on uncovered food they may multiply and cause the food to go bad.

Many of these microorganisms will make the food smell, taste or look unpleasant. Other bacteria that contaminate food are very dangerous, but may not give us the warnings of a nasty smell or a bad taste.

Other microorganisms can cause food poisoning if the contaminated food is eaten. Salmonella is a bacterium which, if eaten in large numbers, will cause fever symptoms, diarrhoea and sickness. The Salmonella bacterium is killed by heat.

Food lasts longer if it is kept cold. Refrigeration slows down the rate at which bacteria multiply, so they cannot break food down quickly.

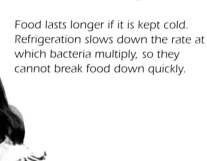

- Here are some statements about safe cooking. Why are they true?
- Pre-prepared food should always be cooked at a temperature of over 100°C.
- Food should not be kept warm for a long period of time.
- Frozen chickens should always be completely thawed before cooking.

Some foods are heat-treated so that they keep longer. What does the heating do?

Gone off!

Resazurin is a blue dye which changes colour in sour milk.

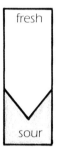

- Label your test-tubes A, B, C.
- Put 10 cm³ of fresh pasteurised milk into A.
- Put 10 cm³ of 2 day old pasteurised milk into B.
- Put 10 cm³ of 4 day old pasteurised milk into C.
- Put 1 cm³ of Resazurin into each test-tube.
- Cork the tubes and shake them well.
- Put the tubes into a beaker of warm water (about 45°C).
- Observe and record any colour changes in a table like the one below.
- How fresh is each sample?
- Bacteria make the milk go off. How do you think the bacteria get into the milk?
- What does the test tell you about the number of bacteria in each sample?
- In what ways could you keep milk fresh for as long as possible?
- Why do you think you were told to use 10 cm³ each time?

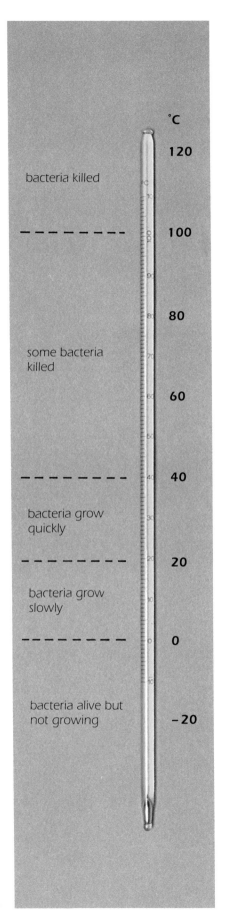

Colour after ... minutes	Milk samples		
	A	B	C
0			
1			
5			
10			
20			
30			

Floating and flying

Have you ever wondered why it is that some things float and others don't?

When a boat floats, two **forces** act on it. One force acting on the boat is **weight**. Weight pulls the boat down. The second force is called **upthrust**. This is a force pushing upwards on the boat. Normally, the weight is balanced by the upthrust.

Although it may seem strange, similar ideas apply to a boat on water, to an aeroplane in the air and to a car on the ground!

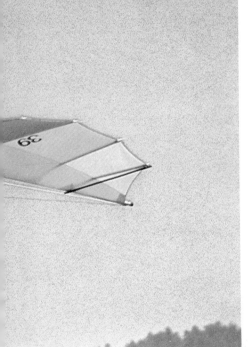

Keeping opposing forces in balance is just as important for the hang glider as it is for an aeroplane – if it wants to remain in the air!

The more effectively the downwards force of the hang glider's total weight is balanced against the upwards force, (lift) the longer it will stay airborne.

Thor Heyerdahl's raft was called *Kon-Tiki*, after a legendary ruler of the ancient Inca kingdom of South America

Float a raft

A raft is a simple kind of boat. An explorer called Thor Heyerdahl believed that in the past people might have travelled across the Pacific Ocean on rafts from South America to Tahiti. In 1950, to try and prove his hypothesis, he and five friends travelled 6920 km across the Pacific on a balsa wood raft like the one in the picture below.

As an aeroplane moves through the air, the shape of its wing means that there is an upwards force called **lift** acting on it. This force just balances the downwards force of the aeroplane's weight.
- Discuss what you think would happen if the lift force was reduced.

The weight of a car is exactly balanced by an upwards force called the **reaction**, produced by whatever surface the car is on.

- Use kitchen foil to make a raft.
- Devise a way to load and test the raft.
- What is the greatest load your raft will carry without sinking?
- Devise a way to report the results of your tests, including how you loaded the raft.
- Write a letter to Thor Heyerdahl explaining to him the best way to load the food and provisions for his expedition. In your letter, you should explain the reasons why his raft will float if he loads it in the way you suggest.

How does it go?

Have you ever tried rowing a boat on a lake or river?

■ Discuss with your friends how you felt after rowing.

Moving a boat (or anything else) needs **energy**. In the case of the rowing boat, you provided the energy, which is why you felt tired afterwards. You were the energy source.

■ The boat in the picture below does not have oars. What is its energy source?

One of the oldest sources of energy drives these yachts.
What is it?

Fuel

Some boats have engines to make them move. Engines need **fuel** as the energy source. What is the usual energy source for a boat engine?

Most modern ships use fuel oil. For ships, this has many of the advantages that petrol has for the motor car.

■ Discuss what these advantages might be.

A few large ships such as aircraft carriers and some submarines use nuclear fuel as an energy source. A small amount of fuel will last for a long time, so the ship doesn't have to come into harbour to refuel. A submarine, therefore, can stay hidden under the water for a long time.

MOVE IT!

How does the force of the wind affect the movement of a raft? These children have set up a simple experiment to find out

Sailing boats

We have seen that we can make things that float and sink, but how can we get a raft to move?

■ Look at the picture of the raft on spread 3.1.

■ How do you think the force of the wind and the direction of the wind will affect the movement of the raft?

■ Make a plan to test your idea.

■ Show your teacher your plan and then carry it out.

■ Record your observations.
Was your idea correct?

Did you know?

● There is enough petrol in a full tank of a jumbo jet to drive an average car four times round the world.

● If we all boiled one less kettle of water each day, we would save 4000 tons of fuel a week.

3.3

Going faster!

So far, you have been investigating how sailing rafts move through the water. Most modern boats are not raft-shaped, however.

■ Look at the three boats in the picture.
■ Discuss with your friends which moves through the water most easily, and why?
■ You may have found it difficult to answer the question. The picture does not show a fair test. Why is that?

When an object moves and rubs against something else, a force called friction acts to slow the object down.

■ Discuss how friction acts to slow your bicycle when you stop pedalling.

Moving boats are also affected by friction. Friction between the boat and the water tends to slow the boat down.

■ How do the people who build boats try to reduce friction?
■ Carry out the investigation on **copymaster 6**.

MOVE IT!

Faster sailing boats!

- Your task is to design a small sailing boat that will go as fast as possible.
- Start by sketching out a design on paper.
- Choose materials from the selection provided to make your boat.
- Discuss your ideas with a partner to see if you can think of as many ways as possible of getting your boat to move through the water faster.

Your teacher will show you how the boat is going to be moved through the water. You will need to decide at the start of the activity what you are going to measure to see which design of boat moves fastest.

- Write a report to include a table of the measurements you have made.

Weight is a force

Gravity is a force which acts on all things, pulling them towards the Earth. It is this force which makes things feel heavy.

Mass and weight

The amount of matter in you, the Earth and everything else is measured in grams and kilograms. This is called the mass of the object. The pull of gravity towards the Earth on a mass causes a downwards force. We call this force its weight.

Gravity pulls on a 100 g apple with a force of about 1 N. The apple's weight is about 1 N.

Sir Isaac Newton

The idea of gravity pulling on objects was first proposed by a famous British scientist called Sir Isaac Newton (1642–1727). There is a well-known story that when Newton was sitting in his garden, he noticed an apple fall to the ground. As he was a good scientist, he made an hypothesis that the apple fell because it was pulled to the Earth by a force.

From the hypothesis, Newton developed his famous theory of gravitation, that the force of gravity acts on everything – the Moon, you and the apple!

In his honour, forces are measured in units called **newtons**, (abbreviated to N). The story may or may not be true, but it might help you to remember that the pull of gravity on a small apple is about 1 N. This means that the weight of the apple is about 1 N.

We use an instrument called a **newtonmeter** to measure forces.

MOVE IT!

Measuring forces

- Use newtonmeters to measure the force needed to do the sort of tasks shown in the pictures.
- Make sure that you use the correct newtonmeter for each different task.
- Make a table to record your measurements.

Inside structures

The Eiffel Tower soars 303 m above
Paris, France. It was built in 1889 by
Alexandre Eiffel, a brilliant engineer

It may be hard to believe, but all materials change shape when forces act on them. The changes that take place in a block of concrete or a steel girder are often so small that they are difficult to see with the eye.

■ Discuss with your friends what happens to the Eiffel Tower when the wind blows.

If an object changes shape when a force is applied and then goes back to the same size and shape when the force is removed, it is said to be **elastic**.

The **load** on the beam in the picture on the opposite page is the weight of the elephanr plus the weight of the beam itself. The load causes the beam to bend. Inside the beam:

● the top surface is pressed inwards, or is in **compression**

● the centre is least affected

● the bottom surface is pulled outwards, or is in **tension**.

■ Discuss this with your teacher.

Something being pressed inwards is said to be 'in compression'.
Something being pulled outwards is said to be 'in tension'

70

MOVE IT!

Testing the beam

■ Carry out an investigation to find out what affects the load which can be carried by a simple beam.

Investigating springs

■ Set up the apparatus as in the diagram.
■ Measure the length of the spring.
■ Add a load of 1 N to the spring.
■ Measure how much longer the spring is (how much it has stretched).

■ Repeat these steps and increase the load by a small amount each time.
■ Record your results in a table like the one below.
■ Draw a graph of the load on the spring against the increase in its length.

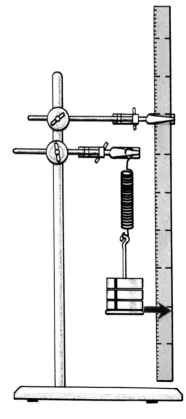

Load (N)	Length of spring (cm)	Increase in length of spring (cm)
0		
1		

Bridging the gap

Engineers and scientists use special words to describe how forces act on and affect structures such as bridges.

If we push a structure, then we say it is in compression. The forces are trying to squash it.

If we pull a structure, we say it is in tension. The forces are trying to stretch it.

Types of bridge

Here are three types of bridge.

Beam bridge
Lay a plank of wood across a stream and you have a beam bridge. If the beam is supported at each end by uprights which project towards the middle, it is a cantilever bridge.

Arch
Quite small blocks of stone are shaped carefully to fit tightly together. All the stone blocks in an arch are in compression. Stone is good at resisting compression.

Suspension bridge
Cables are used to support a flat deck (the road). The support cables pass over the towers and down to anchorages. The cables are in tension and the towers are in compression.

For a successful bridge, both the design and the choice of materials are important.

Beam bridge

Arch bridge

Suspension bridge

MOVE IT!

AMAZING NEW MATERIALS FOUN[

English scientists today announced the discovery of two amazing new materials that could revolutionize the whole construction industry.

Rumour has been rife in the manufacturing industry for some years now heralding the arrival of exciting new materials. In fact, it has been said that its properties are so unusual that the ...ill probably never

Switzerland to discuss some of the many fundamental problems inherent in the industry's most important building materials. Weight, flammability, strength, resitance to wear and tear were just some of the areas covered with reference to specific materials.

scientific specialist should be approached and entrusted with the task of developing new materials that would meet the ever increasing demands of both politicians and environmentalists.

So after a decade of toil by the scientists, the secret's finally out - announced with all the razzmatazz of the launch of a new political party. Called nottoc and ittehgaps, the new materials show an increase in torsional strength of more than 200% while redu...

Testing materials

Scientists have discovered two new materials but not enough is known about their suitability for building bridges! The materials are nottoc and ittehgaps.

- In the next activity, you will use nottoc and ittehgaps to build a bridge. Try to plan and carry out compression and tension tests on both the new materials.
- You will need to measure and record the forces used to test the materials.
- Write a full report of your tests on **copymasters 8 and 9.**

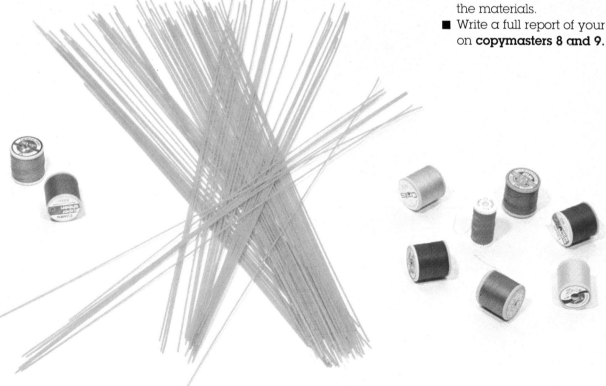

Two bridges across the Forth

The picture shows the cantilever bridge which spans the Firth of Forth in Scotland. When completed in 1890, the bridge carried two railway lines across the Firth of Forth and spanned 1631 m. A workforce of 4500 took 7 years to build it. There were 57 fatal accidents during construction. The design used 50 000 tonnes of steel and 8 million rivets. More than 54 tonnes of paint are needed. It takes three years to paint, and when painting is finished it is time to start again.

When a new road bridge across the Forth was needed in the 1960s, engineers were more skilful and had better materials to use. They were able to design and construct a suspension bridge next to the cantilever bridge. The towers rise to 158 m and support cables made of many thousands of steel wires. Only 250 people were employed to build this bridge. It used only 30 000 tonnes of steel.

■ Look carefully at both photographs.
■ Discuss the differences between the two bridges. What shape is used on the rail bridge and why? Which parts of the suspension bridge are in tension and which in compression?

The 1890 Firth of Forth bridge

MOVE IT!

Build a bridge

- Your task is to design and construct a bridge to span the length of a laboratory storage tray. You may choose any design of bridge.
- There must be at least 4 cm clearance under the bridge for a boat to pass through.
- It must support a load of 10 N (a 1 kg mass) at mid-span.
- Your design must be cost-effective (good value for money).
- Work out how much your bridge has cost to build.

Price List

Nottoc ....£2000 per metre

Ittehgaps ....£1000 per length

Hire of............£500 per day or
  glue gun   part thereof

Glue sticks.......£2000 per stick

Card ....£5000 per sheet

The new Firth of Forth bridge

75

On the move

People have always had a need to travel.

■ Discuss with your friends some reasons for this. In your discussions, you should consider the sorts of vehicles that people used in the past as well as those we use today.

■ What are the differences between early vehicles and modern vehicles?

Speed

Modern vehicles travel much faster. The **speed** of boats and cars is measured in different units. Car speedometers in England and the USA are usually marked in miles per hour (mph). See if you can find out what units are used to measure the speed of boats. In France and most other countries in the world, speed is measured in kilometres per hour (km/h).

To calculate the speed of something, we need to know two things about it:
● the distance it travels
● the time it takes to travel that distance.

If we measure distance in miles and time in hours then the units of speed will be miles per hour. If we measure distance in metres and time in seconds, what would the units of speed be?

All vehicles should have a means of stopping quickly. How do you do this on your bicycle? The speed you are travelling affects the time and distance it takes to stop. If you need to stop quickly, you have to pull the brake lever much harder to exert a larger stopping force.

MOVE IT!

Traffic survey

- Your task is to plan and carry out with a friend a traffic speed survey near your school. You need to know how far the vehicles travel and the time it takes them to cover this distance. It may be helpful to use trees or lamp posts as markers for this activity.

- Select appropriate measuring instruments for the task.
- Draw a table like the one below and record your measurements for each vehicle that passes.
- To work out speed, use a calculator to divide distance by time:

$$\text{speed} = \text{distance} \div \text{time}$$

- Fill in the last column of your table with your results.
- Write a report on your traffic speed survey.
- Read the information on **copymaster 11** and answer the questions on it.

Type of vehicle	Distance between markers (m)	Time to travel between markers (s)	Speed (m/s)

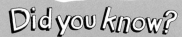

SAFETY ⚠️

When you carry out your survey, be sure that you are safe from all the traffic. Make sure that your teacher knows exactly where you will be at all times.

Did you know?

The world's fastest car is the rocket-powered *Budweiser Rocket*. On 17 December 1979, it was driven by American Stan Barratt at over 1190 km/h (739 mph), which is faster than the speed of sound.

Traffic in Hong Kong

Moving energy to where it's needed

Think about a person riding a bicycle. Where does the energy to move the bicycle and rider come from?

■ Discuss this with your friends. When you pedal a bicycle, you apply the pushing force to the pedal, yet the force is needed at the wheel to make the bicycle move along. How does the energy you supply get from the pedal to the wheel?

In cars, energy is supplied in the form of petrol or diesel. A pipe takes the liquid fuel to the engine, where it is burnt to release the energy to turn the wheels. This energy is passed through a series of gears (in the gearbox) and along metal shafts (driveshafts) to the wheels.

MOVE IT!

You may have used technical Lego to make models move. You may have needed to move energy from one part of your model to another. To do this you will have used gears, rubber bands or shafts.

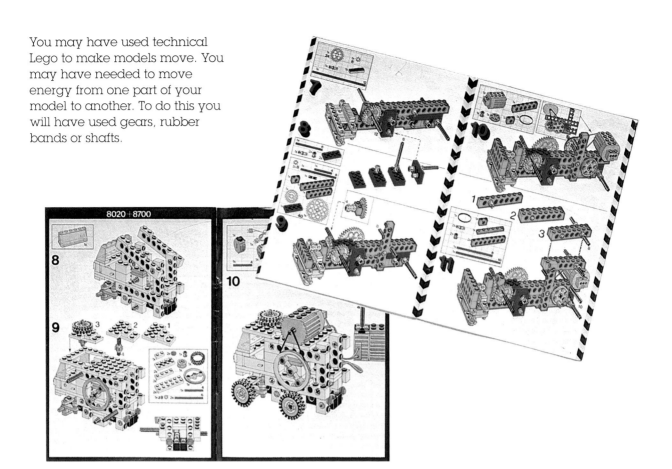

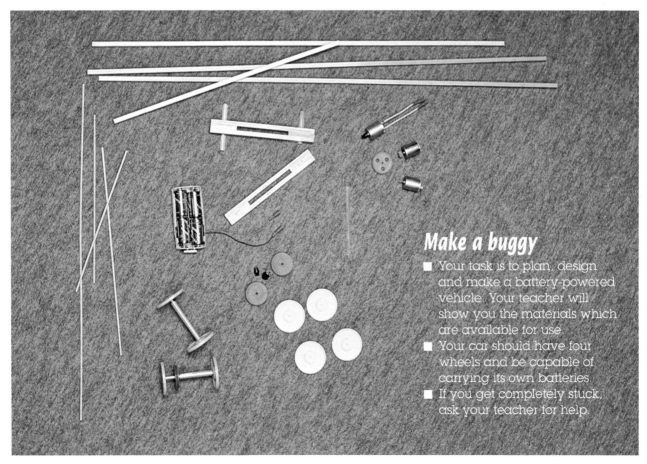

Make a buggy

■ Your task is to plan, design and make a battery-powered vehicle. Your teacher will show you the materials which are available for use.

■ Your car should have four wheels and be capable of carrying its own batteries.

■ If you get completely stuck, ask your teacher for help.

That sinking feeling

Have you ever tried to ride your bike in soft sand, snow or mud? Maybe you have been in a car that has become stuck in soft ground. When people have to drive on snow, they often let some of the air out of the tyres of the car. What does this do to the shape of the tyre and to the area of the tyre in contact with the ground? Why doesn't a skier sink into soft snow?

■ Discuss with your friends what might be the advantage of letting some air out of car tyres when driving on snow.

■ Look at the picture on the next page. Why doesn't a bulldozer sink easily into soft ground?

MOVE IT!

A giant bulldozer moves easily through soft mud

Buggies investigated

- Try to find out what affects the movement of your buggy.
- Adapt your vehicle so that it can cross a tray full of sand.
- Report what you have found out.

Turning forces

Forces which try to turn things, such as the force of the wind on the boat and the crew's weight, are called turning forces.
When you open a door, you use a turning force on the handle. We call this the **effort**. The force you overcome is known as the **load**. The distance from the effort to the turning point (or **pivot**) affects the size of the force needed to do the job. In the picture, the weight of the boy being lifted is the load.

■ Look at the photograph.
■ Discuss why the boat does not capsize, even though the wind is trying to push it over.

■ How have the boat crew increased the distance of the effort force from the turning point?
■ Look at the pictures below with your friends and decide in each case where the effort force, load and pivot are. One picture has been labelled to help you.

Lift a friend!

■ Use a long piece of wood and a piece of broom handle to set up an arrangement like that shown in the picture.
■ Apply an effort force at the end of the plank. This time, apply the effort force closer to the pivot.
■ Describe what you noticed in trying to lift your friend. Where is it easiest to apply the force successfully?

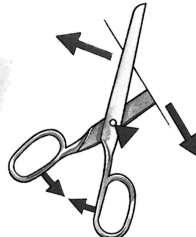

MOVE IT!

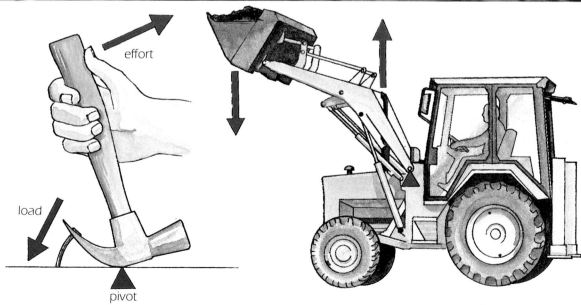

effort

load

pivot

Going up?

Astronaut Harrison Schmitt collecting rocks on the Moon during the Apollo 17 mission in 1972

The launch of Apollo 11 – the first mission carrying people to the Moon taking off from the Kennedy Space Center, USA, on 16 July 1969

Every planet and star has its own different force of gravity. The size of the gravity force depends upon what the planet is made of and its size. The force of gravity on the Earth is about six times bigger than on the Moon.

■ Discuss with your friends the direction in which gravity would act if you were on the surface of the Moon.

■ Report your group's ideas to the class.

Remember the story of Isaac Newton and how watching an apple fall helped him to make an hypothesis about a force called gravity? What would happen if gravity suddenly ceased to exist?

Which way would an apple fall if you lived in Australia? You might never have been to Australia but even so, you can still be pretty sure of your answer! Will the answer always be the same wherever you live on the Earth's surface or will it vary from place to place?

You may have seen someone using a plumbline when hanging wallpaper. What force is pulling the plumbline straight down towards the floor? Gravity does the same thing to the apple and the plumbline. It always pulls things in the same direction, towards the centre of the Earth.

So far, we have been talking about gravity on our own planet.

MOVE IT!

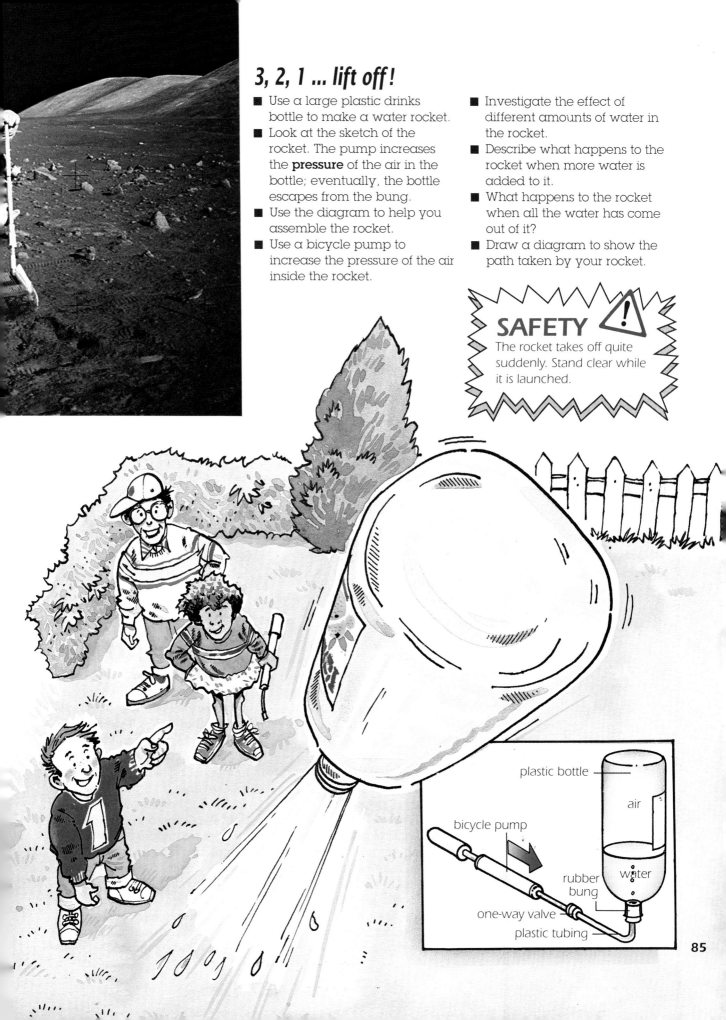

3, 2, 1 ... lift off!

- Use a large plastic drinks bottle to make a water rocket.
- Look at the sketch of the rocket. The pump increases the **pressure** of the air in the bottle; eventually, the bottle escapes from the bung.
- Use the diagram to help you assemble the rocket.
- Use a bicycle pump to increase the pressure of the air inside the rocket.
- Investigate the effect of different amounts of water in the rocket.
- Describe what happens to the rocket when more water is added to it.
- What happens to the rocket when all the water has come out of it?
- Draw a diagram to show the path taken by your rocket.

SAFETY ⚠
The rocket takes off quite suddenly. Stand clear while it is launched.

plastic bottle

air

bicycle pump

rubber bung

water

one-way valve

plastic tubing

Living and changing

A changing environment

The environment is the area where plants and animals (including humans) live. There are lots of particular places, or localities, in the environment. The grounds around your school provide many examples:

● the playing field
● lawns
● flower beds
● the cracks between paving slabs.

Animals and plants depend on each other in many different ways. For example, plants can give shelter to animals. Some types of bird build their nests in hedges, others prefer to use trees, while skylarks nest on the ground in open meadows.

Competition for life

Living things are in competition with each other for the things necessary for life. These include light, water and soil space. Can you think of any others? The winners in this competition live longer. Plants which don't receive enough light or animals which don't obtain enough water from their environment, for example, may die out completely and become extinct – either locally or worldwide.

■ Can you think of some examples of animals or plants which have become extinct, or are perhaps in danger of becoming extinct?

Investigate the school grounds

In your first activity, you will explore your local environment – the grounds around your school.

Outside the laboratory
■ Work in groups of two or three.
■ Record the names of at least 10 different living things that you have found in the school grounds, but which you have never noticed before.
■ Look for and collect 10 leaves each from a different plant in the school grounds.
■ Make a list recording the names of any animals with wings that you can see around the school.

Inside the laboratory
■ Sort your leaves into these two groups according to their appearance: put leaves of similar lengths into the same group; regroup the leaves depending on their shape (e.g. oval leaves, rounded leaves, leaves with smooth edges, leaves with 'saw-toothed' edges etc).
■ Sort the list of winged animals that you have already seen and recorded into the following two groups: animals with backbones, or vertebrates; animals without backbones, or invertebrates. (These animals sometimes have hard outer cases called exoskeletons which protect the soft inner parts.)
■ What effect do you think the largest leaves will have on any plants and animals living underneath them?
■ Are most of the plants that you have found similar in one way which you can see easily?
■ Did you find one group of plants which were very different in appearance? If so, what was the difference?

No environment remains the same all the time; there is continuous change. Sometimes, these changes take place very slowly. Other changes take place once or several times within a 24-hour cycle.
■ Can you think of some of these environmental changes which occur every day?

4.2 Biological keys

No-one can remember the name of every animal or plant. There are far too many of them. However, scientists frequently need to be able to identify different living things.

Searching through books full of descriptions and pictures would take a long time. It is much quicker to use a biological key to help solve this problem.

A biological key asks a series of questions about the organism which is being studied. The route which you take through the steps of a key depends upon the answers to the questions.

Eventually, the key leads to the name of the organism.

Using the external features of a plant or an animal, it is possible to put plants into their major groups: non-flowering or flowering; and animals into their major groups: invertebrates or vertebrates.

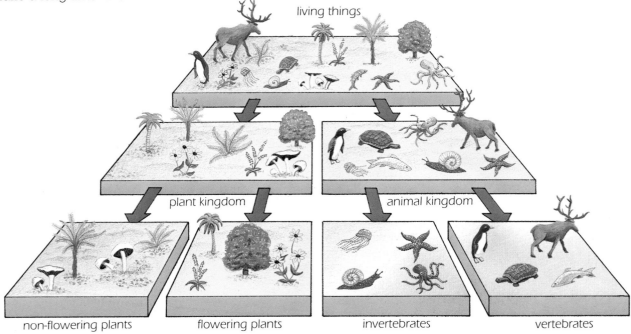

living things

plant kingdom   animal kingdom

non-flowering plants   flowering plants   invertebrates   vertebrates

■ Look at these vertebrate animals and then see if you can use the key below to name them.

Key			
1 A	(If) the animal has scales (go to)		**2**
B	(If) the animal does not have scales (go to)		**3**
2 A	(If) the animal has dry scales (it is a)		**Lizard**
B	(If) the animal has wet scales and fins (it is a)		**Trout**
3 A	(If) the animal has feathers (it is a)		**Bird**
B	(If) the animal has fur (it is a)		**Hare**

Using a key

On **copymaster 2** you will find pictures of various invertebrates.

■ Use the key below to find the names of these animals.

A key to some common invertebrates

1	A	The animal has legs or tentacles	**4**
	B	The animal does not have legs or tentacles	**2**
2	A	The animal has a coiled shell	**Snail**
	B	The animal has no obvious shell	**3**
3	A	The body is made up of segments	**Earthworm**
	B	The body has no segments	**Flatworm**
4	A	The animal has three pairs of legs	**5**
	B	The animal has more than three pairs of legs or tentacles	**7**
5	A	The animal has one pair of wings, large compound eyes, short antennae	**Housefly**
	B	The animal has two pairs of wings	**6**
6	A	The animal has a slender body which is longer than the wings	**Damselfly**
	B	The body is shorter than the wings, the tail has two prongs	**Stonefly**
7	A	The animal has eight legs or tentacles	**8**
	B	The animal has more than eight legs	**9**
8	A	The animal has eight tentacles and has an unsegmented body	**Octopus**
	B	The animal has eight legs and a segmented body	**Mite**
9	A	The animal has five pairs of legs, the front two ending in claws	**Crab**
	B	The animal has more than five pairs of legs	**10**
10	A	There is one pair of legs to every body segment	**Centipede**
	B	There is more than one pair of legs to every body segment	**Millipede**

Making a key

■ Your task is to make a key to identify four animals of your own choice. For each animal, make a list of its features, for example does it have fur or scales, how many legs does it have? Use these features to write a key which other people could use to identify your animals.

89

Who eats whom?

Some animals only eat plants, for example the caterpillars which live on cabbage leaves. These animals are called **herbivores**. Some animals eat other animals. Blackbirds and thrushes, for example, eat caterpillars, snails and worms. These animals are called **carnivores.** Animals which eat both plants and animals are called **omnivores.**

■ Think about the variety of foods you eat. To which group do humans belong? We have a special name for animals which hunt and feed on other animals. They are called **predators**. The animals which are eaten are called the **prey.**

The way in which predators, prey and green plants fit together in an environment can be shown as a food chain.

An example of a simple food chain in the garden:

> **green plants**
> eaten by
> **herbivores**
> eaten by
> **carnivores**

greenflies
eaten by **ladybirds**

rose bush
plant juices sucked out by **greenflies**

The hunting game

This game involves a series of hunts made by a pride of lions which are preying on a population of antelopes living in Moremi National Park.
You will need **copymaster 5**.

Rules of the game

■ Work in pairs. One person takes the part of the lions and the other takes the part of the antelopes.

■ Antelopes start with a population of 30. They hide in the squares of the National Park. Mark 30 squares lightly with a pencil to show their distribution. Do not let your partner see where they are.

■ Lions begin with a pride of three lions.

■ Lions hunt by naming a number from 1 to 50. If there is an antelope in this square, it is rubbed out because the hunt is successful. If there is no antelope in this square, the hunt is unsuccessful. Lions must keep a record on rough paper of successful and unsuccessful hunts.

■ A round of hunting means that each lion has one guess at where an antelope is hiding in the Park.

■ After each round of hunting, the number of successful and unsuccessful hunts is added up and the populations are changed like this: for every successful hunt, one extra lion is added to the pride; for every two *unsuccessful* hunts, one lion is removed from the pride due to starvation; two extra antelopes are added after every round because of reproduction. (Remember to mark these on your plan of the National Park.)

■ The results must be recorded after every round in a table like this:

Round of hunting	Number of lions	Number of antelopes
Start	3	30
1	2	

Example

Imagine a game where, after 3 rounds, there are 7 lions and 22 antelopes. In the next round there are 4 successful and 3 unsuccessful hunts. Because of the successful hunts, 4 extra lions are added but 1 lion is removed because of the unsuccessful hunts.

The new lion population = 7 + 4 − 1 = 10

In addition, 4 antelopes were killed but 2 are added every round due to reproduction.

The new antelope population = 22 − 4 + 2 = 20

■ Continue for up to 20 rounds of hunting.

■ At the end of the game: Has the balance between predator and prey changed during the game? Did the skill of the hunters affect the relationship?

Same or Different?

No two individuals of the same type, or species, are exactly the same. Even identical twins have some differences. Biologists call the differences between individual animals or plants **variations**. The overall variation between individuals is caused by both genetic and environmental variation.

Genetic variations

These differences are present at the start of life. They are inherited from the parent plants or animals and can be passed on to the next generation. For example, the colour of the eyes of a fruit fly depends upon the colour of the eyes of the parent fruit flies.

■ Are there any similarities or differences, for example hair colour, which have been inherited throughout the members of your family?

In what ways are these twins similar? In what ways are they different?

Which plant grew in the dark?

Environmental variations

These differences are not present at the start of life but are caused by conditions in the local environment. Examples of such conditions include varying amounts of light, water supply and differences in the available soil minerals.

For example, a plant grown in the dark will be very different from a plant grown in full sunlight, even if both plants were grown from cuttings taken from the same parent. Both plants inherited exactly the same features, so in theory they should be identical. They look different because different environmental conditions have caused variation in their growth.

LIVING AND CHANGING

Why is variation important?

Variation is important for survival. A species in which every individual is identical and which is perfectly adapted to its environment will be successful. If, however, there is a sudden change in environmental conditions, for example a change from a wet to a dry climate, then the species will probably die out in that locality.

If some individuals are slightly different from the rest and are able to tolerate the new, drier climate, the species will survive.

Selective breeding

Variation is also important in selective breeding programmes. Horticulturists try to find individuals which have useful characteristics, for example short stem height in wheat plants. The short-stemmed individuals can be used to produce offspring with even shorter stems.

This kind of work has led to the development of dwarf wheat varieties. These have saved money for farmers because they do not blow over in strong winds.

Measuring variation

Fitzlyker Ltd, the famous glove manufacturers, want to start a new line of children's safety gloves for use in school laboratories. They have decided to concentrate on the 10–12 year old market.

The production manager believes that children of this age all have hands of about the same size. Therefore, it is only necessary to make one size of glove to fit every child.

The research director thinks that the amount of variation in hand size is so great that the company will have to make gloves of several different sizes.

Fitzlyker Ltd have decided to call in a firm of consultants to discover who is correct.

- Imagine that you are the consultants. Your task is to find out if there is a variation in hand size. You will, therefore, be able to recommend what size of gloves should be made.
- Make an hypothesis about variation in hand size – an hypothesis is an idea with a reason. Plan how you will investigate any variation in the size of hands of the children in your class.
- Carry out your plan. What measurements will you have to take? How will you record your results?

Interpreting your results

- When you have recorded your results, draw a bar chart using the axes shown below.
- Discuss your results with the others. Is there much variation of hand size in your class?
- Was your hypothesis correct? Would you advise Fitzlyker Ltd to make only one size of glove or a range of sizes?
- Write a letter to the production manager of Fitzlyker Ltd recommending how many sizes of glove the company should make. In your letter, you should give: details of how you carried out your investigation; all the reasons, including your results, which support the recommendations you have made.

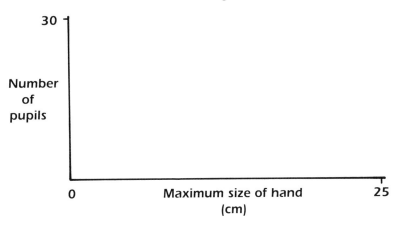

A place to live

If you went on a long journey from the Arctic to Antarctica, you would pass through many different environments. You could go from the polar ice-cap, through northern pine forests, grasslands, alpine meadows, deserts and many other areas.

While on this journey, you would notice many changes in the environment. The climate would range from the permanently frozen Arctic or Antarctic to the steamy heat of the tropical rain forests.

The landscape would include mountains and valleys, flat plains, gently rolling hills, rivers, lakes and seas. The soils would also vary widely in both depth and richness.

You would notice that, as you passed from one type of environment to the next, the types of plants and animals in the area also changed.

The animals, such as antelopes, which live in the African Savannah (grasslands) would be out of place in the Arctic Circle, and polar bears are certainly not found in Africa.

94 ■ Why do you think this is?

Parts of the world which have similar environments have similar plants and animals. The plants which you would see high up in the colder regions of the Alps are similar to those found in the Arctic Circle. They are called Arctic–Alpine plants.

In later activities, you will be investigating whether different types of animals are found in different environments around your school. You will be thinking about why animals and plants live where they do.

Finding out about soil animals

- Your task is to investigate the numbers and types of animals in soil from two different localities: under short, trampled grass; under leaf litter or dead wood.

Outside the laboratory

- Work in groups of two or three.

In each area:
- Clear the surface of the soil and take a small sample. One trowel-full should be enough.
- Place the sample in a labelled plastic bag. Take it with you to the laboratory.

- Record the temperature of the soil both at the surface, and at a depth of 5 cm.
  You will have to use a special soil thermometer or an electronic sensor.
- Write a brief description of the location.

> *Always treat living things with care and return them to their habitat at the end of the lesson.*

Inside the laboratory

For each soil sample:
- Count and record the total number of soil animals found.
- Use the key on **copymaster 9** to try to identify the animals and count the number of each type of animal. Record your observations.
- Mix a small amount of soil with some distilled water in a test-tube. Filter the suspension using a funnel and paper. Collect the filtrate in another test-tube. Test the pH of this filtrate using a strip of universal indicator paper. Record your results.
- Was there a difference in the total number of animals found in the two different soil samples?

- Were there differences in the types of animals found in each area?
- Discuss with your partner(s), the possible reasons for any of the differences that you have discovered (e.g. soil pH, temperature, shading, or any other cause that you can think of). Record your ideas.
- If you were to sample the same area next week, next month or even next year, would you expect to get the same results? Explain the reasons for your answer.

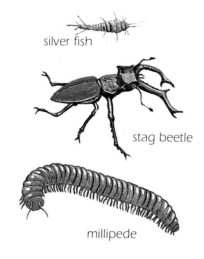

silver fish

stag beetle

millipede

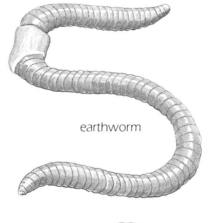

earthworm

slug

Features for survival

The fennec fox, which lives in the Sahara desert, is adapted for life in hot climates. Its large ears act as radiators and give off excess heat

To survive, animals and plants must be adapted to the locality in which they live.

Plants living in the cracks in a pavement must grow as close to the surface of the concrete as possible. What would happen to a plant if it continued to increase its height on a busy pavement with many people passing by?

A similar danger faces plants growing on a lawn which is mowed regularly. Successful broad-leaved plants such as daisies and dandelions survive by growing close to the soil. They often grow as a tightly packed group of leaves called a rosette.

Survival in deserts

Animals and plants which live in deserts have many special adaptations allowing them to live in a hot, dry environment.

Desert plants have long roots to obtain water from deep below ground. They have a shiny layer of wax over their stem to reduce water loss and small leaves, or only spines. These spines also reduce water loss because they have a small surface area.

■ In what other ways do spines help desert plants to survive?

Cacti are a typical group of plants which live in deserts.

Mammals that live in deserts often have large ears. Some of the body heat produced during movement and digestion is lost from these large surfaces.

■ Do you think that mammals which live in the Arctic and Antarctic will also have large ears and long tails?

LIVING AND CHANGING

Camouflage

The colour of the animal can also be important in helping it to survive. Colours and patterns which help an animal to merge into its surroundings are called **camouflage**. Camouflage helps some of the prey animals to hide from their predators.

■ How do body colours help the hunters to survive?

Some animals actually change their colour at different times of the year. The willow grouse and ptarmigan are two game birds from northern Europe. They grow white feathers for the winter. The stoat and the Arctic fox are two predatory mammals which live in the same geographical region. They grow white fur.

■ What is the advantage of this seasonal colour change for creatures which live in or near the Arctic Circle?

Woodcock fledglings camouflaged among leaves

Design a creature

You have looked at some ways in which animals and plants are adapted to survive in different places, including the environment outside your school.

The picture below shows a different environment – a deep, dark swamp on the imaginary planet of Kulmarnus. The climate is hot and steamy. There is hardly any oxygen in the atmosphere. The short 'day' is equal to four hours on planet Earth. Darkness at night lasts three times as long.

■ Your task is to design a 'life form' (an animal or plant) which would be well adapted for survival on Kulmarnus.

■ Make a large, fully labelled drawing of your 'life form'. Any adaptations or special features for survival should be explained clearly.

The changing seasons

No environment always stays the same. In North Africa, the Sahara desert has the highest recorded 'shade' temperature anywhere on Earth, 58°C. At night, temperatures in deserts drop sharply and they become very cold.

On Earth, changes occur in temperature between day and night and also throughout the year during the four seasons: winter, spring, summer and autumn.

Plants and animals respond to seasonal changes in many different ways. Deciduous trees lose their leaves in autumn. Most deciduous trees have 'broad leaves' which have a large surface area.

■ How would a heavy fall of snow affect the branches of deciduous trees, if they kept their leaves throughout the winter?

How animals adapt

Some animals, including British bats and North American bears, sleep or hibernate through the cold months of winter. Other animals avoid unfavourable seasonal conditions by travelling or migrating from one part of the world to another.

■ Can you think of any examples of vertebrates and invertebrates which migrate?

In addition to these longer-lasting seasonal changes, the regular changes of day and night take place every 24 hours.

Animals which are active by day are called **diurnal**, for example humming birds. Animals which are active at night are called **nocturnal**. British bats hunt at night.

■ What sort of differences would you expect in the external appearance of diurnal and nocturnal animals?

Many animals hide away to sleep, or hibernate, during the cold winter months

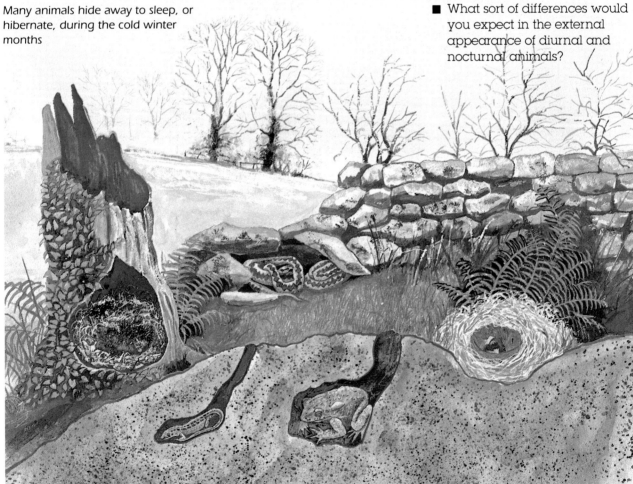

Some examples of seasonal animal migration. In which season do you see swallows, swifts and cuckoos in Britain?

■ Carry out the investigation on **copymaster 10**.

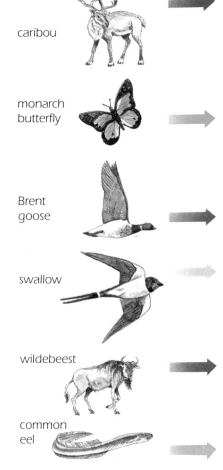

caribou

monarch butterfly

Brent goose

swallow

wildebeest

common eel

The Negev desert in Israel during the dry season (below). The same scene after rain (right) is full of colour as flowers bloom

Sources of pollution

Most of the things people do alter the environment in some way or other. Some of these changes can be harmful to the lives of all plants and animals.

Sea and air pollution

Changes might be easy to see. For example, the black crude oil washed on to a beach from a leaking tanker at sea is obvious.

Other changes caused by humans are less obvious. One of the changes that we can't see is the release of carbon dioxide into the atmosphere.

■ Why do you think that we can't see carbon dioxide gas?

The damaging effects of escaping oil quickly become obvious, but effects of the release of too much carbon dioxide take longer to show. Both types of damage to the environment are known as **pollution**.

Pollution is often the result of the careless things people do or their attitude. 'It's someone else's problem,' they say. However, we all breathe the same air which circulates around the world in the atmosphere. The water in the seas and oceans is also a shared natural resource. Therefore, the poisoning of the sea and the air affects us all.

Land pollution

The land can also be polluted. Everyone produces rubbish such as paper and cardboard packaging, empty glass bottles and metal cans. Some of these materials get spread about at refuse tips or are deliberately dumped in the countryside by thoughtless people. Do you always put your empty crisp packets in a litter bin?

■ During the next break or lunchtime, look around the school grounds to see if this type of pollution is a problem in your local environment.

What evidence of pollution is there in the photograph?

LIVING AND CHANGING

Detecting and preventing pollution

Pollution occurs in the air, in water and on land. Your task is to investigate an example of each type of pollution.

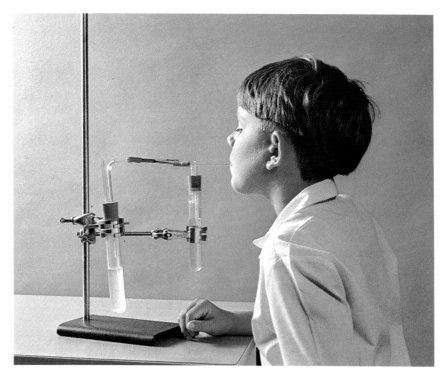

Air pollution: investigating carbon dioxide

The amount of carbon dioxide in the atmosphere can be increased by:

● animal and plant respiration
● burning fuels such as coal, wood and petrol.

The test for carbon dioxide is that it turns lime water milky.

■ Does the air we breathe out contain more carbon dioxide than the air we breathe in? Use the apparatus shown above to investigate this question. Record your observations.
■ Does a burning candle produce carbon dioxide? Investigate this problem using the apparatus below and record your observations.

Water pollution: investigating the effects of oil

The most common type of oil pollution is caused by mineral oil. This oil is extracted from the ground.

■ Take three 250 cm^3 beakers and put 100 cm^3 of water into each one. Pour oil on to the water to a depth of 5 mm. What happens?
■ What effect do you think a layer of floating oil will have on the plants and animals living in a rock pool on the beach or under the water in a canal?
■ How can you disperse or sink this oil?
■ Add a few drops of washing-up liquid to the first beaker. What happens?
■ Drop powdered chalk on to the film of oil in the second of your beakers. What happens to the oil?
■ If you add sawdust to the film of oil in the third beaker, what happens? Would you be able to scoop up this oil and sawdust mixture from the surface of polluted water?
■ From your experimental results, which of these three methods would you recommend to prevent the spread of oil pollution on areas of water?
■ Write a report of your findings.

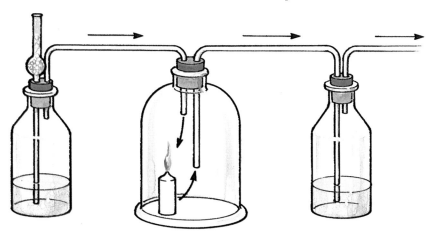

Land pollution: unwanted rubbish

■ In groups of two or three, discuss if there is a litter problem in your local environment. If you think there is, what can you do to solve the problem? Are more litter bins the answer?
■ Can you educate the polluters about the damage they are doing to the environment?
■ Would you ban eating snacks at break time?

4.9

The Foxley Mound plan

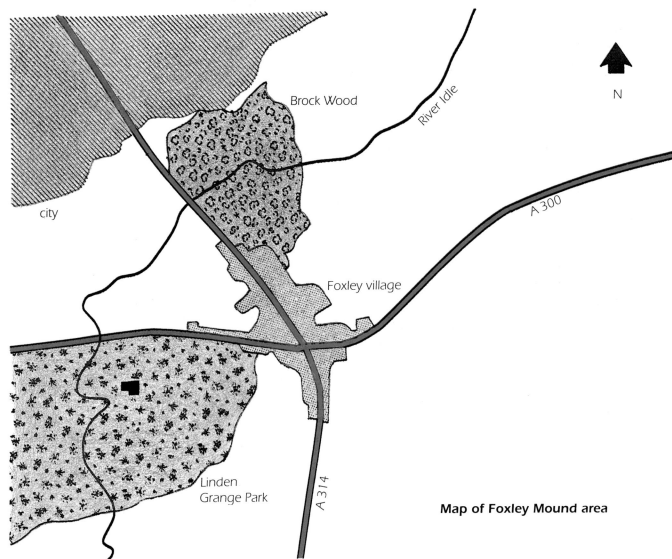

Map of Foxley Mound area

The county of Ruralshire lies in central England. The county contains a major city where more jobs and houses are needed, together with shopping and leisure facilities for the people. The local authority Planning Department has identified that Foxley can provide these.

Foxley is a medium-sized village set in high quality agricultural land. Two main roads run through the village,

creating a traffic problem. The local authority believes a by-pass will solve this problem.

In return for permission to build houses, shops and the industrial park, the developer will provide a leisure complex and by-pass.

Objections to the plan

However, there have been many objections to the plan from existing residents of Foxley. They are worried about the size of the

new development, the increase in traffic and noise, and the loss of part of Linden Grange Park. Linden Grange house is of great historic and architectural interest. The park contains many trees which are specially preserved and, with Brock Wood, provides an important habitat for plants and animals.

A public inquiry is held for everyone to put forward their views both for and against the Local Plan.

The public inquiry

■ In groups of five, your next activity is to take part in the public inquiry into the Foxley Mound Local Plan. Decide who is going to play each of these roles:

Inspector – controls the inquiry

District Planning Officer – explains and supports the plan and reports on views put forward to the Secretary of State for the Environment

Chairperson of Richly Investments – supports the plan

Conservationist – objects to parts of the plan

Residents' Committee Representative – objects to parts of the plan.

■ When you have decided on your roles, each person must read the information provided for their particular part on **copymaster 12**.

■ The Inspector will open the inquiry. You may wish to take notes as other people are speaking or record the inquiry using an audio tape recorder or camcorder.

■ After the inquiry has taken place and everyone has had the opportunity to speak, a *complete* report has to be written, based on the evidence for and against the plan. The Secretary of State for the Environment decides whether the plan will be accepted, altered or rejected. It is most important, therefore, that your record presents the all evidence as accurately as possible.

■ In your report, you should include the following information:

● the main changes which will occur in the environment, if the original plan goes ahead unaltered;

● if you support the plan, you must say why you think it is a good idea;

● if you think that the plan should be changed, you must explain what these changes are and why you think they are important;

● if you think the plan should be rejected, explain why.

Foxley Mound Local Plan

This map shows the planning proposals for the by-pass, new industry, houses, hypermarket and leisure complex. A new 'green area' will separate Foxley from the city.

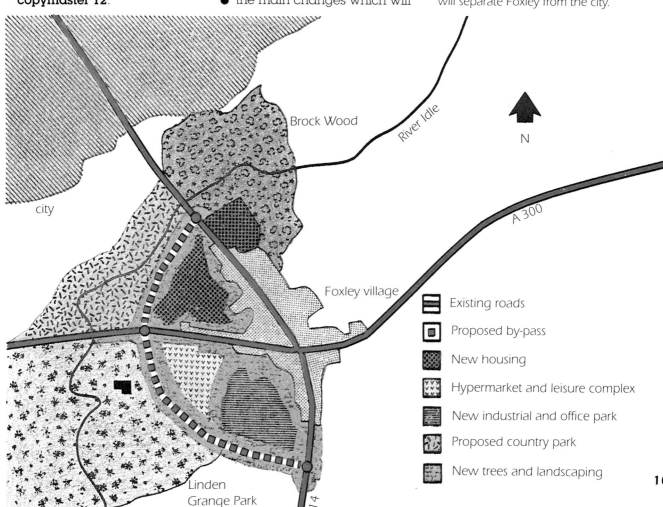

Brock Wood
River Idle
N
city
A 300
Foxley village

Existing roads
Proposed by-pass
New housing
Hypermarket and leisure complex
New industrial and office park
Proposed country park
New trees and landscaping

Linden Grange Park
A 314

A better future?

The fox adapts easily to town life as cities spread into the countryside. Unfortunately not all animals are as adaptable

You have seen that the environment doesn't remain the same all the time.

Some changes take place every 24 hours, for example night turns into day. There are also slower changes over several months. In Britain, the weather in each of the four seasons is different, for example. Such patterns of change are not the same everywhere.

Altering the balance

You have also investigated how plants and animals depend on each other. In particular, you have seen how the way in which animals feed and hunt can alter the balance in their environment.

However, the biggest changes to the environment are brought about by humans.

■ Can you think of some examples where human activities completely alter the environment?

Is there a balance between the human activities which are good for the environment and those which damage it?

What can you do?

There are many things you can do at school and at home to improve the environment. You will look now at a few examples which would help to ensure a better future for everyone.

LIVING AND CHANGING

In your school

- Design, produce and distribute posters to inform and educate about environmental problems. Are there other types of pollution requiring attention as well as those investigated in spread 4.8?
- Take part in school competitions such as those organised by Shell Better Britain and the World Wide Fund for Nature.
- Organise the recycling of valuable resources to help the environment: collect and recycle old newspapers; collect and recycle aluminium cans; set up a bottle bank to recycle glass.
- Construct a chequerboard arrangement of paving slabs and different soil types such as sandy soil, clay, loam and rapidly draining pebbles. You can then grow colonies of specially adapted plants.
- Build and/or maintain a school pond or a wild garden.
- Give an account of what you have done.

How does using products like these help the environment?

Outside school

- Join local groups and societies which undertake practical environmental projects and publish further information in newsletters and magazines, for example: the Royal Society for the Protection of Birds; the local County Naturalist Trust and their junior wing, 'Watch'.

Conservation work can be fun!

Glossary

This glossary explains the meaning of important words as they are used in this book. As you understand more about science, you will find some of the meanings may change. They may also change as you meet the words in different situations.

accelerate
getting faster

acid
a sour-tasting, corrosive chemical; an acid solution has a pH of less than 7

algae
simple, very small plants

alkali
an alkaline solution has a pH of greater than 7 and can neutralise (cancel out) an acid

alloy
a mixture of two or more metals

artery
a blood vessel which carries blood away from the heart

atoms
the tiny particles that matter is made of

bacteria
a microorganism made up of a single cell

biomass
the total mass of living things in an environment

camouflage
colours and markings on an animal similar to its surroundings

capillary
a narrow blood vessel with thin walls which allow oxygen and dissolved food to pass through

carbohydrate
a type of food which provides energy

carbon dioxide
a colourless gas found in small amounts in the air

carnivore
an animal which eats other animals

cell
the tiny unit of which all living things are made

cell membrane
the thin skin around a cell

cell wall
the rigid wall around a plant cell

chlorophyll
the green pigment in plants which absorbs light energy from the Sun during photosynthesis

chloroplast
the parts of a plant cell that contain chlorophyll

chromatography
a way of separating soluble pigments

classify
to group together things according to their properties and features

compression
a squashing or pushing force

condensation
the process of changing a gas into a liquid by cooling

cytoplasm
the clear, jelly-like substance found inside cells

density
the amount of matter in a certain volume

digestion
the process by which food is broken down and made soluble so that it can pass into the blood

diurnal
active during the day

dormant
inactive

effort
the force used to lift a load

elastic
a material is elastic when it returns to its original shape when any force acting on it is removed

energy
the ability to do work

environment
the area where animals and plants live

enzyme
a substance produced by living things which changes the speed of chemical reactions, such as those occurring during digestion

ephemeral plant
a plant which has a very short life

evaporation
the change of a liquid to a gas without boiling

exoskeleton
a skeleton which is outside the body

fat
a food which provides energy

filter
a very fine strainer used to separate insoluble solids from liquids

filtrate
the liquid that passes through a filter

food chain
a series or line of living things, each of which is the food for the next in line

food pyramid
a diagram showing which animals feed on plants and which on other animals

food test
a test to determine the content of foods

force
a push or a pull

friction
a force that slows down moving objects that rub against other objects

fuel
a substance which releases energy on burning

genetic variation
the differences between individuals of the same type which are present at birth

germinate
to start growing into a plant

gravity
a force of attraction between objects caused by their mass, which pulls objects closer together

herbivore
an animal which feeds on plants

indicator
a chemical that changes colour when added to an acid or alkali

insoluble
does not dissolve

invertebrate
an animal which does not possess a backbone

lift
the upwards force on, for example, the wings of an aeroplane due to its movement through the air

load
the weight carried by a beam, or the force overcome by a lever or other machine

localities
the particular places where plants and animals live

lubricant
a substance used between two surfaces to make them slide over each other more easily

mass
the amount of matter in an object, measured in grams and kilograms

matter or **material**
what everything is made of

microorganism
a very small organism that can only be seen through a microscope

mineral
an essential substance for growth of living organisms

neutral solution
a solution which is neither an acid nor an alkali

newton
the unit of force

newtonmeter
an instrument used to measure the size of forces in newtons

nocturnal
active during the night

nucleus
the part of a cell which controls everything going on in the cell

omnivore
an animal which feeds on plants and animals

organ
a group of different types of tissues with a particular job to do

organ system
a group of organs

organism
a living plant or animal

pathogen
an organism that causes disease

pH scale
a scale of numbers that shows how strongly acidic or alkaline a chemical is

photosynthesis
the process by which plants make their food

pigment
a substance that gives colour to things

pivot
a turning point

pollution
damage to the environment caused, for example, by poisonous materials

predator
an animal which hunts and eats other animals

pressure
the force acting over a given area

prey
the animals hunted and eaten by predators

property
a feature used to describe and identify a material

protein
a substance found in some food which is used for growth and repair

reaction
a force that is the same size but in the opposite direction to another force

residue
the solid which a filter separates from a mixture

respiration
the process by which energy is produced from simple food substances

solubility
how easily something dissolves

soluble substance
a substance that dissolves

solute
the solid that dissolves in a solvent to make a solution

solution
the mixture obtained by dissolving a solute in a solvent

solvent
the liquid that dissolves a substance

species
a group of animals or plants that can breed among themselves

speed
the distance covered in a given time

states of matter
the different forms of matter: solid, liquid, gas

tension
a stretching or pulling force

thermometer
an instrument for measuring temperature

tissue
a group of the same types of cells

upthrust
the upwards force acting on an object in a liquid or gas

vacuole
a fluid-filled sac inside a cell

variation
the differences between individuals in a group of the same animals or plants

vein
a blood vessel which carries blood to the heart

velocity
speed in a given direction

vertebrate
an animal with a backbone, and a skull surrounding its brain

vibrate
move rapidly back and forth

virus
a tiny organism that lives in the cells of plants and animals

vitamin
a substance found in food which is needed in small amounts for health

volume
the space taken up by a solid object, liquid or gas in three dimensions

weight
the downwards force pulling an object towards the Earth

Index

Acknowledgements

The co-ordinators would like to acknowledge the help and support given to them in the development of *New Horizons: science 5–16* by their teaching and advisory colleagues in West Sussex. They would like to thank the following schools for providing valuable assistance in the production of this book: Buckingham Middle School, Shoreham; Boundstone Community College, Lancing; Imberhorne School, East Grinstead; Oathall Community College, Haywards Heath; St Paul's RC School, Haywards Heath; Thomas Bennett Community College, Crawley.

The authors and publishers would like to thank Usborne Publishing Ltd for permission to reproduce the 'eating machine' illustration (pp 40–1) from *How Your Body Works*.

Photographic credits

t = top   *b* = bottom   *c* = centre   *l* = left   *r* = right

Cover: Allsport UK

8*b*, 8*t*, Science Photo Library; 9*t* ZEFA; 10*l*, 12, 14/15, 17, 18*tl*, 18*tr*, 18*cr*, 19, 20*t*, 20*b* Trevor Hill; 21 ZEFA; 22/23*c*, 23*br*, 24/25*t*, 26, 27 Trevor Hill; 32/33, 35 Allsport UK; 36 Planet Earth Pictures; 38/39 Trevor Hill; 42/43 ZEFA; 42*l* Planet Earth Pictures; 42*r* Science Photo Library; 43*l*, 43*r* ZEFA; 46*b* Trevor Hill; 48 Science Photo Library; 49, 50, 51 Trevor Hill; 52*t* ZEFA; 52/53*b*, 53*tl* Trevor Hill; 53*tr* Image; 53*br* Sally and Richard Greenhill; 55*l* Science Photo Library; 55*r*, 56 Trevor Hill; 58*b*, 59*t* Science Photo Library; 60, 61*r* Trevor Hill; 62*t* ZEFA; 62*b* Allsport UK; 64 ZEFA; 65 Trevor Hill; 70 ZEFA; 73*b* Trevor Hill; 74 Chris Fairclough Colour Library; 74 ZEFA; 76*t* Mansell Collection; 77 ZEFA; 78 Allsport UK; 79*t*, 79*c*, 79*b* Trevor Hill; 80, 81*t* ZEFA; 81*b* Trevor Hill; 82*t*/83*t* ZEFA; 84*l*, 84/85*t* Science Photo Library; 87*b* Trevor Hill; 92*t* Chris Fairclough Colour Library; 94*tr* ZEFA; 94*tl*, 94*cl*, 94*cr*, 94*b* Planet Earth Pictures; 95*b* Trevor Hill; 97*t* Planet Earth Pictures; 99*l*, 99*r* Frank Lane Picture Agency; 100 ZEFA; 100*t* Trevor Hill; 104 Planet Earth Pictures; 105*t*, 105*b* Trevor Hill.

Published by the Press Syndicate of the
University of Cambridge
The Pitt Building, Trumpington Street,
Cambridge CB2 1RP
40 West 20th Street, New York, NY 10011-4211, USA
10 Stamford Road, Oakleigh, Victoria 3166, Australia

© West Sussex County Council 1991

A catalogue for this book is available from the British Library

ISBN 0 521 43548 X

First published as Y7 Pupil's Book 1991

This second edition published 1993

Designed by Pardoe Blacker Publishing Ltd, Shawlands Court,
Newchapel Road, Lingfield,
Surrey RH7 6BL
Illustrated by Annabelle Brend, Dawn Brend, Neil Bulpitt, Chris Forsey,
Mike Gordon, John Hutchinson, Frank Kennard, Jenny Mumford, Keith
Palmer, Peter Sarsen, Jon Williams, Paul Williams
Indexed by Indexing Specialists, 202 Church Road, Hove, East Sussex
BN3 2DJ

Printed and bound in Spain by Mateu Cromo, S.A.